CALLY ON THE BALL

CALLY
ON THE BALL

Sport Media

With John Keith

This book is dedicated to the memory of my late, lovely wife Linda, to my two daughters – Samantha and her partner John and Suzanne and her husband Danny – and to my grand-daughters Eve and Lilli.

Ian Callaghan, April 2010

Ian was not only a superb footballer and exemplary role model but I am proud to say he has also been a great friend of mine for many years, and it's been a delight to co-operate with him in producing this book.

John Keith, April 2010

CALLY ON THE BALL
By Ian Callaghan with John Keith

Production: Michael Haydock and Lee Ashun

Produced by Trinity Mirror Sport Media:
Business Development Director: Mark Dickinson. Executive Editor: Ken Rogers.
Senior Editor: Steve Hanrahan. Senior Production Editor: Paul Dove. Senior Art Editor: Rick Cooke.
Sales and Marketing Manager: Elizabeth Morgan.
Sales and Marketing Assistant: Karen Cadman.

Sub Editors: Roy Gilfoyle, Adam Oldfield, Michael Haydock.
Designers: Barry Parker, Colin Sumpter, Lee Ashun, Glen Hind, Alison Gilliland,
Jamie Dunmore, James Kenyon, Lisa Critchley.
Writers: Chris McLoughlin, Simon Hughes, John Hynes, Alan Jewell,
William Hughes.

ISBN: 9781906802455

Photographs:
Courtesy of Trinity Mirror (Mirrorpix/Liverpool Daily Post & Echo),
PA Pics, Ian Callaghan collection

Printed and bound in the UK by
CPI Mackays, Chatham ME5 8TD

Contents

Contents continued

Bottom's continued

When Carra met Cally

I'm proud to hold the record for the number of Liverpool appearances – 857. I was one of those players described immortally by Bill Shankly as a 'marathon man'. When I was asked to meet and have a chat with Anfield's modern-day equivalent Jamie Carragher (600-plus games and eager for more), I was only too happy to oblige. This is what we said when we came face to face at the club's famous training headquarters, Melwood. John Keith sat in on a fascinating conversation.

John: *Can I ask each of you what qualities are needed to put together hundreds and hundreds of games for Liverpool as you've both done, knowing of course that fortune in steering clear of injuries is a big factor.*

Carra: You've just taken away my answer there! (Laughter)

Cally: Yes, you've got to have that bit of luck but you've got to be consistent and you have more games today. There's a squad system today which wasn't there when I played. Then, if you played well enough and consistently enough, you played week in week out, so for you to get through more than 600 games shows how well you've played.

Carra: Obviously, Ian must have been lucky, like me. But saying that, I don't know whether it is just luck. Is it the way we look after ourselves as well as freedom from injuries? To play for that length of time at the top level is not just about playing, it's how you approach it mentally as well.

Cally: That's right. It is.

Carra: There's always people wanting to take your place. It's a bit different now with squads and clubs looking all over the world for players. But you can probably look at that both ways. Years ago if you were in the team you were in it, but I suppose if you went out of the team it was probably difficult to get back in again. The teams were sort of set, weren't they? Whereas, now, if you go out of the team there's always the chance that the manager might change it and get you back in.

Cally: It was like that. I think that's probably why in my day the lads would play carrying knocks which we kept quiet about, because you knew that if you went out there'd be someone to take your place. And you wouldn't get back in.

John: *Would you do the same today, Jamie?*

Carra: To be honest, I think I've come back from injury probably a little bit early at times and not performed as well as I'd have liked.

Cally: That's because you can't wait to play.

Carra: It's also that you're terrified of someone taking your place. One day it will happen but I want to go on for as long as possible.

Cally: That won't be for a long time yet.

John: *Another big factor, Jamie, must be enthusiasm. You must keep your appetite for the game to be able to string together all those appearances.*

Carra: Yes, of course, not only to play that long at that level but to do it for one club, Liverpool. Some players feel they want a change, they need something different, maybe a different manager or different ideas. Not many players go past 600 games for one club.

Cally: I'm not just saying this Jamie, but you can plainly see your appetite and enthusiasm whenever you play. You demonstrate it the way you respond to the other lads in the team. You're chatting to them, pointing where they should go, pulling them into position – you're doing all sorts. That's the way you are… that's your nature.

Carra: I suppose the two of us were born with that. I don't think it's something people can tell you or coach you. I think you've either got that enthusiasm for the game or will to win, or will to keep going, or you haven't. It certainly helps. There's also the

fighting spirit side of things. You and me are different types of players, but at a big club like Liverpool, who are always on the lookout for new players, there's always been someone to take your place, so to be able to stay there and withstand that competition is a great testimony to both of us, I would say.

John: *I think it was Gerard Houllier who, talking about you, Jamie, and Steven Gerrard, said that local players are the heart of Liverpool. I presume you, too, believe that it's important to have local lads at a club like Liverpool.*

Carra: Oh, yes, of course. But it is getting more difficult now with players coming in from all over the world. You have to keep up with the best. But when Stevie and I have gone in the next four or five years, or whatever it will be, it is important that we start bringing young people through because a lot of the success this club has had over the years has been down to local players.

Cally: You and Stevie have been the most consistent players at this club over the past seven or eight years or more. Without a doubt. That's proved by the number of appearances you've both made. For consistency I think you've both been unbelievable, especially given the way the game has changed with all the foreign players here now.

John: *That, Jamie, must make it even more of a challenge for local players to force their way through.*

Carra: Yes, it does, but the game's always changing. That's the challenge for them. When I got into the team it was different from when Ian got in. The foreigners were just starting to come.

Cally: Foreigners to us, Jamie, were the Irish, Scottish and Welsh! (Laughter).

Carra: But I'm sure, Ian, that if you were playing today, whatever was put in front of you would have been a challenge you'd face and come through it. You'd get into the team. One way or the other you'd find a way. That's the attitude and mentality you've got.

John: *Jamie, you and Steven Gerrard came through at Liverpool before the Academy was introduced, while Ian began as an amateur training twice a week here at Melwood. Has the Academy* *system still to prove itself or is it the right way to go?*

Carra: I think it is the right way. I'm not just talking about Liverpool but generally. I think Alex Ferguson's talked about the problem where you can only sign players within an hour's journey of the club's Academy. That's maybe forced clubs to look abroad a bit more. You'd think maybe it should be more the other way to encourage English boys. As I say, though, if you get a good, young foreign player who's fantastic then everyone's happy, aren't they? But there have been a few changes at the Academy and I think over the next few years it is important that we get players through. Most of the foreign players speak English no problem. That's the way the game is and we have to adapt to it. It can't just be different for Liverpool. That's the way football is now with players from all over the world. Wasn't Avi Cohen one of Liverpool's first foreign players?

Cally: Yes, he was an Israeli international signed in 1979, a year after I left Liverpool.

John: *Apart from the influx of South African players, before and after the Second World War, Avi was Liverpool's first overseas recruit.*

Carra: When local players do get in the team they're not looking to leave, really. This is the pinnacle for them.

Cally: If you've grown up watching Liverpool and supporting them, as I did, and then find yourself playing for them, there's a great sense of pride.

John: *Does it put any extra pressure on local lads playing for the club and being part of the community?*

Carra: Maybe a little bit. But on the emotional side you probably feel it even greater when you win and worse when you lose.

Cally: Yes, the emotion of it is stronger.

Carra: Istanbul must have been great for our foreign players, but for me and Stevie, our families and friends, it was just unbelievable.

Cally: That night will be a highlight of your career, Jamie, just like Rome in 1977, when we won the European Cup for the first time, and our first FA Cup win in 1965 are mine. You're making history for the club and making history for yourself.

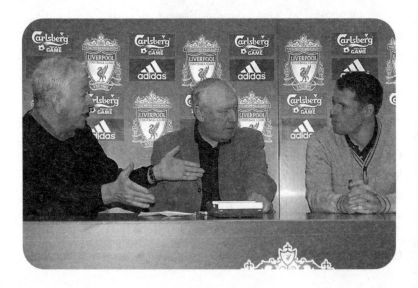

John: *Istanbul was like another "first" because it had been 21 years since Liverpool had last lifted the European Cup.*

Carra: Yes, it had been a long wait for us.

Cally: There will never be another night like Istanbul and we've done a chapter in the book explaining why! It was fantastic.

John: *Do you still pinch yourself, Jamie, whenever you think about Istanbul?*

Carra: To be honest, when you're still playing you're still looking ahead. Perhaps it was the same for you Ian in 1977. It's something to look back on when I finish and think: "That was some achievement!"

Cally: Exactly. What made Rome even sweeter was the fact that we had the horrible disappointment of losing the FA Cup final to Manchester United on the Saturday, which ended our hopes of landing a treble. The fans, as well as the players, had to pick themselves up and cheer all over again against Moenchengladbach. What a fantastic sight it was to see that mass of our supporters in the Olympic Stadium, and what a night for all of us!

Carra: I've seen film of you turning away, not daring to look when Phil Neal took his penalty.

Cally: Yes, I was like this (puts his hands together as if in prayer). (Laughter from Carra)

Carra: I've seen many video clips and highlights of that match. Wasn't it Simonsen who scored for them?

Cally: Yes, Allan Simonsen, the Dane who was European Player of the Year, equalised before my room-mate Tommy Smith headed us back in front and Phil clinched our win from the spot.

John: *Jamie, you have a great interest and knowledge of the game outside of playing for Liverpool, don't you?*

Carra: I always like to watch the old footballers and I also like statistics about the game. I just remember things.

Cally: I'm not like that. I'm very forgetful... and I didn't head the ball a lot either! (Laughter).

John: *I presume, Jamie, your family would have told you about*

Ian's generation of players, your dad being an Evertonian.

Carra: My dad has always appreciated good football. I always think about Ian's team and Bill Shankly. That's where it started for Liverpool and without them it wouldn't have gone on to where it is today. What happened in the late 1950s and 1960s established us as a top club forever, really. One of the biggest clubs in the world. I think the top clubs now will always be the top clubs… Liverpool, Manchester United, Arsenal will always be there.

Cally: When I come to the games I always walk in through the Shankly Gates, and every time I think: "This guy Shanks started it all off." And he did. Liverpool were going nowhere until Shanks arrived. He just grabbed the club by the scruff of the neck. They broke the mould after they made Bill Shankly.

John: *Then, after Shanks, came Bob Paisley. Another fantastic manager. I suppose, Jamie, you'd have liked to have met these people.*

Carra: Oh, I'd have loved to. That's what the club's about, those type of people. It would have been great to meet Bill Shankly. He was a one-off, wasn't he? I got the CD one Christmas of Shankly talking when he was doing his autobiography all those years ago. There's something special about his voice.

Cally: You were scared of him, really. If he came out of his office and walked past you you'd be bowing! There was a fear factor.

John: *Is there a fear factor with managers in football now, Jamie?*

Carra: I think managers have changed. I don't think it's like that now. Maybe the odd one or two at different clubs. None of the three managers I've had at Liverpool (Roy Evans, Gerard Houllier and Rafael Benitez) have ranted or raved. They earned respect but didn't scare people. That's the modern game. You could probably take it a bit more, Ian, than some of the players can these days.

John: *The rewards for players now are greater than they were in Ian's day. Has money affected the game?*

Carra: Yes, I think it probably has. People talk about players in the old days having no power or freedom of contract but now it's gone totally the other way and probably a balance somewhere in the middle would be better for the game in general.

John: *I think it's given a problem to the man in the street because it's hard for him to identify with players now.*

Carra: Of course it is. That's why me and Stevie, as local lads with our friends and family around us, always know someone locally who can be a link to the team. Hopefully, in a few years we'll have more local lads coming through because without them it would seriously affect the relationship between the man in the street and the players.

Cally: I entirely agree with that. But as a local it doesn't just affect you. Your missus has to go to the butchers, your children have to go to school and if the team hasn't done well they'll get a bit of flak.

Carra: I've had that myself!

John: *Were you both conscious of the importance of being role models and setting examples?*

Carra: Yes, I think so, especially as you get older. I'm the oldest in the squad now so I feel I have to set an example not just outside but also in the dressing room. Players coming through have to know the standards required for Liverpool, not just on the pitch but off the pitch as well. I think it is important that older players do that and that it's not just down to the manager.

Cally: Having role models is so important now because football is so high profile today. It wasn't anything like that when I played. You couldn't do the things today that some players of my generation got up to.

John: *Jamie, how do you feel about the intense media interest today?*

Carra: I enjoy talking about football and doing interviews. I think it works both ways. You probably get more praise than you deserve when it's going well and more the other way when it's not going well. Maybe years ago it was a bit more balanced. I don't know. Now it's sensationalised either way. So if you enjoy the good press in the good times, telling you how great you are, you've got to accept it the other way and take it on the chin.

Cally: I don't know how I'd deal with it but I do know the media spotlight on the game is very different from my day, like so many

other things… the game's so much quicker, the pitches are so much better, the ball's lighter. Football's been transformed.

John: *What are your views on goal-line technology, given FIFA's decision to reject it?*

Carra: Football's the biggest game in the world and every other sport has introduced new technology so maybe we should, especially for really big decisions.

Cally: We had a classsic example this season of the ball clearly crossing the Portsmouth goal-line in their FA Cup win over

Birmingham. Yet the goal wasn't given. But I don't think we should meddle with the game very much even though some changes – like the back pass to the goalkeeper – have been great. Football is still the best game in the world and it's not like rugby where you can stop and start. Football's not like that.

Carra: I just wonder how many times we have incidents like the one at Portsmouth, with the question of whether the ball was over or not. How often does it happen? Maybe only four or five times a season.

Cally: Sometimes it can be vital, the difference between a team being relegated or staying up or winning or losing a trophy. But when it comes to technology I would tread warily.

John: *Finally, can I ask you Jamie if you could ever envisage anyone approaching Ian's record 857 appearances for Liverpool?*

Carra: No, I can't. When I think of you, Ian, playing all the way from the old Second Division all the way to a European Cup final… that's some achievement. And I'm still trying to work out how you made 857 appearances! My target is to reach 700 – and then I'd be second to you.

Cally: I hope you make it. In today's game the number of appearances you've made already is a fantastic feat.

On tour in the USA with Liverpool in 1964 – I ended up playing there when I left Anfield

Life after Liverpool – with George Best for a room-mate!

There is a football life after leaving Liverpool and I thoroughly enjoyed mine.

Nothing, of course, can ever replace or match wearing that red jersey, and after 857 appearances for the club it was quite a wrench when the parting of the ways came for me in 1978 at the age of 36.

Swansea City and Crewe Alexandra – as well as Fort Lauderdale in Florida, Canberra City in Australia and Cork Hibernians in Ireland – all provided memorable moments for me before I finally hung up my boots.

But I should have added another club to that list. And it still baffles me as to why it never happened. In the spring of 1981, after I'd finished a two-and-a-half-year spell with Swansea and played a couple of games for Cork, I was approached by a representative of Norwegian club Sandefjord.

I flew over to meet him and although it was only a small,

part-time club, it was situated in a beautiful part of the world, about 100 miles south of Oslo, with some spectacular seascapes.

The guy who negotiated with me also ran sports shops and the idea was that as well as playing I would do some public promotional appearances for his business. There was no problem with that, everything was agreed and I was looking forward to it.

Then I heard the shock news that my work permit application had been rejected by the Norwegian authorities.

I would have thought that having played for Liverpool, being included in England's World Cup-winning squad and collecting a host of medals would have fulfilled any criteria. But they turned me down and never explained why. To this day I don't know the reason.

A seat on the Wembley substitutes' bench, watching the team beat Bruges to retain the European Cup in May 1978 – which also brought me my second winner's medal in the competition – was my last act of duty for Liverpool.

The next morning I flew out to Florida to join Fort Lauderdale for the summer, officially on loan from Liverpool although I never kicked another ball for the club.

I had a great time in the States where my wife Lin, daughters Suzanne and Samantha and I lived in the same apartments as former Everton player Gary Jones, who had signed permanently for Lauderdale from Birmingham. I'd only been out there for a few weeks when the Lauderdale coach and former Portsmouth, Leyton Orient, Crystal Palace and Gillingham winger Ron Newman came to me and said: "We're signing George Best from Los Angeles Aztecs. What do you think?"

"Fantastic," I replied. "George is, without doubt, the best player I've ever seen." And I meant that. I didn't see Pele or Maradona very often. But I saw a lot of George – and played against him many times – and for me he's the most gifted of them all.

I don't know whether Ron thought that George needed a steadying influence, but when he arrived he asked him to room with me on club trips. What a great guy – and he could still play, too! He'd just married Angie, who got on well with my wife Lin. George did go missing a few times to go back to LA, but despite the thousands of tons of newsprint and hours of film and TV footage he generated, he was essentially a quiet guy who was great company. And I can honestly say I never saw him the worse for drink in that entire summer. In fact, he conducted himself superbly.

During that close season here, my Anfield room-mate Tommy Smith had agreed to play for our former team-mate John Toshack who had taken over as player-manager of Swansea City, then in the old Third Division. Smithy arranged for me to join him there if I fancied the idea. I think he wanted someone to accompany him on the trips to South Wales and I agreed to go after having a chat with Bob Paisley.

Bob was terrific about the whole thing. He offered me a new contract but told me quite honestly that with Graeme Souness there I wouldn't be playing many games. Bob left it entirely to me.

I felt I had a few years left in me, so in September 1978 I signed for Tosh and joined a small "colony" of former Liverpool players at the Vetch Field. As well as Tosh, Tommy and me, centre-forward Alan Waddle was there as well as Phil Boersma.

I played in 40 of the 46 league games that season and Tommy played in 36 to help Swansea to promotion into Division Two. Tosh asked me to sign for another season, which I agreed to do.

But that summer of 1979 I went out with the family to play for

Canberra City, and what a wonderful experience it was. The purpose-built Australian national capital was constructed in the early part of the 20th century, and it's beautifully laid out.

The city is full of diplomats and we lived in some style in the New Zealand High Commissioner's house for the four-and-a-half months we were there.

The team was a mixture of amateurs and semi-professionals who trained at night, and the club was sponsored by Dunlop. So I wore Dunlop boots and travelled all over Australia promoting them as part of the deal I'd agreed.

I returned to Swansea for the 1979/80 season, by which time Tommy had become a coach after hanging up his boots, and I made 36 appearances as the club finished mid-table.

I didn't play again for the Swansea first team. I got an Achilles' tendon injury for which I was treated at Liverpool. One day Tosh rang me to ask how I was.

I told him I was feeling good and he asked me to go down and play in a reserve game for Swansea. So I drove down and played in this tiny football ground in the pouring rain.

After having a shower and jumping in the car to make the long drive home in the early hours, I thought to myself: "This is it. Call it a day."

When I woke up next morning I rang Tosh and asked if he'd be kind enough to terminate my contract. "No problem," he said. "And thanks very much for your services. It's been brilliant."

I'm glad to say that he and Swansea managed to complete their climb to the top flight at the end of that 1980/81 campaign. But later that season I received an invitation to play a few games for Cork Hibernians in the League of Ireland, which produced a memorable moment at Dublin airport.

I had been unable to get a direct flight, so I flew to Dublin to catch a connection to Cork. I learned that on the flight with me was the great American singer Johnny Mathis and his entourage.

Johnny had been playing in the Howard Keel celebrity golf tournament at Mere in Cheshire and was travelling to play a concert in Dublin.

So at the airport I seized my chance and got him to autograph a book I'd been reading on the flight, signing it to Lin and my two daughters.

Ronnie Moran's 'Yellow Peril' – and cars of the stars

Ronnie Moran was a wonderful servant to Liverpool, spending half a century at the club and filling a variety of roles including player, captain, coach and – in two spells – caretaker manager.

It was a record to be proud of... but I can't say the same about a particular car he owned!

During his playing days as a full-back, he bought a cheap, yellow Morris Minor that didn't have a heater. It was so cold in that car that he used to warm himself up before he got in it! It gave us all a good laugh.

Roger Hunt's choice wasn't much better. He had a Riley Kestrel – a small saloon. Not the sort of modest vehicle you would expect a World Cup hero to drive.

Roger's car was in total contrast to that of another England international, Alan A'Court. Alan, who sadly died while this book was being written, drove the classiest vehicle at the club during my early days – a swish, chocolate-brown Sunbeam Rapier convertible. It was in that car that Alan took me into the centre of Liverpool when I was a young player and helped me open my first bank account.

I earned £10 a week in a brown wage packet when I turned pro and Alan took me down to Barclays Bank, then in Water Street, who were the club's bankers.

To give you an idea of how good that wage was for me at that time, it was an almost three-fold increase on my previous weekly income of £3 and 10 shillings (£3.50 in today's money) as an apprentice central heating engineer.

I still find it hard to believe some of the incredible earnings of some of today's players. In fact, any current Premier League player is banking a sum that the man in the street just cannot comprehend.

I'm not a jealous or envious person, and I certainly wouldn't dream of criticising modern professionals.

The formation of the Premier League in 1992 and the coincidental arrival of satellite television combined to build a money machine that has made millionaires of many players on lucrative contracts... a far cry from the days in the early '60s when the whole of the Liverpool team earned the same.

But I believe I played in a better football era than today, and I wouldn't swap my experiences and my career for anything.

People regularly say to me: "I bet you wish you played today with all the money in the game."

And I tell them bluntly: "No. I don't. I played under the two greatest managers in Shankly and Paisley, helped the club win their first FA Cup and first European Cup, and was a member of the only England squad to win the World Cup."

They look at me in amazement.

The one regret I do have is for players who came before me, whose great skills and talents came before television revolutionised the game in the 1990s, and therefore very little of how our football forefathers played the game is there for posterity.

I'm still delighted that youngsters who've seen me on videos recognise me and ask for my autograph. But I find it sad that very little film exists of legendary players such as those two Merseyside greats Dixie Dean and Billy Liddell, for example.

It would be terrific if you could flick a switch and enable today's and future generations to witness their dazzling skills.

Ray Clemence: Great keeper – who fancied himself as an outfield player

（4）

Picking my
Liverpool no 1s

Around 650 players have pulled on a Liverpool jersey since the club's first match, a Lancashire League home game against Higher Walton on 3 September 1892, which they won 8-0 watched by a crowd of just 200.

I have played alongside and watched a good proportion of those 650 since I made my first-team debut 50 years ago and, in fact, for quite a few years before that on the occasions when I went to Anfield as a young fan.

So to sit down and pick my best Liverpool side is a daunting task. But I took up the challenge – which you will read about as this book unfolds – and reached my decision. Then it came down to naming my top three and, finally, the best Liverpool player of my lifetime. I'm sure my selection – an an adventurous 4-3-3 formation – will start arguments raging among Anfield observers young and old!

The task begins with choosing a goalkeeper. It is a position in which Liverpool have traditionally been strong, prompting the club in days gone by to choose their telegraphic address as "Goalkeeper Anfield".

Before I was around they had great keepers such as Teddy Doig, Sam Hardy, Kenny Campbell and Elisha Scott, and in the title-winning side of 1946/47 the Wales international Cyril Sidlow was first choice.

Those who saw him say that Elisha was the best ever – a view powerfully backed by Everton's legendary centre-forward Dixie Dean, who had famous tussles with the great Irish keeper in the Mersey derbies of the 1920s and 1930s.

The first Liverpool goalkeepers I remember were people such as Dave Underwood, Doug Rudham and Tommy Younger. By the time I signed as a professional and made my debut, Bert Slater was between the posts, followed by Jim Furnell.

But at West Brom in October 1962 a Liverpool goalkeeping dynasty was born when Tommy Lawrence made his debut. Over the course of almost the next quarter-century Lawrence, followed by Ray Clemence and Bruce Grobbelaar, missed only nine games between the three of them – an amazing record of consistency.

The keepers who stood in for them, between Lawrence's debut and Clemence's successor Grobbelaar's first absence from the Liverpool side in August 1986, were Billy Molyneux (one appearance), John Ogston (1), Frank Lane (2) and Steve Ogrizovic (5).

Jose 'Pepe' Reina has also distinguished himself between the posts for Liverpool, and there is no doubting the Spaniard's great qualities. His decision making and shot stopping, particularly when facing penalties, has been impressive.

Tommy Lawrence came through the ranks at Anfield, having joined Liverpool in 1957. One of his tasks on the training ground was to go between the posts when Billy Liddell was doing shooting

Sweeping up at the back: Pepe Reina and Tommy Lawrence

practice. Rather him than me! Billy broke a goalkeeper's hand in a league game such was the ferocity of his kicking.

But Tommy forced his way into the Shankly team and stayed there for years as we won championships, the FA Cup and began the club's record-breaking march through Europe. He was a bulky keeper, earning the unfortunate nickname of 'The Flying Pig', but Tommy was remarkably agile for his size and had a wonderful, philosophical temperament. He was an unsung hero.

Another label Tommy earned – and one that was totally appropriate – was given to him by Joe Mercer after he'd watched his display in our 1966 Charity Shield win over Everton at Goodison. "Today," said Joe, "I have just seen the first ever sweeper-keeper in English football." No doubt he had been struck by the contrast between Tommy's readiness to dash from his line as a last defender and the traditional stay-on-the-line policy employed by previous generations of keepers.

Tommy was fearless and rightly earned his place in Anfield

history – as did Bruce Grobbelaar, who was also a style-setter as the "Clown Prince of Goalkeepers".

Bruce was a showman to his fingertips, which, incidentally, helped him to produce many stunning saves for Liverpool after Bob Paisley had recruited him from Vancouver Whitecaps in 1981 for a mere £250,000.

He played to the gallery with his handstands, mock seagulls on his cap and the time-honoured wobbly-leg tactic in the 1984 European Cup final penalty shoot-out, which led to Roma's Graziani firing over the bar and, ultimately, Joe Fagan's Liverpool side lifting the trophy in their opponents' own stadium.

But in between Tommy and Bruce was the man I consider to be not only the greatest Liverpool goalkeeper of my lifetime but possibly the best anywhere – Ray Clemence. His England rival was Peter Shilton, another fine keeper, and they alternated for England. Clem, though, was the better of the two in my opinion. He was unspectacular but brilliant in his reading of the game, his agility, his shot stopping and, very importantly, his concentration.

Like a lot of keepers, Clem always fancied himself as an outfield player in training. His enthusiasm sometimes ran away with him and Bill Shankly had to rein in him in because his tackling on the training ground could have injured one of us!

But between the posts he was peerless, and his total of 665 Liverpool appearances is the most by any keeper in Liverpool's history, and his total of 323 clean sheets is a club record.

The great Gordon Banks made a telling point when he observed that while Peter Shilton was usually a busy goalkeeper for the teams he played for, Clem often had long spells of inactivity as the last line of our defence and very often had to burst into action from the cold, which demanded the utmost concentration.

Nelson Mandela – and the moment that will live with me forever

There are some experiences that are indelibly marked on my memory. Being part of the Liverpool team that ended the club's 73-year yearning to win the FA Cup in 1965 and lifting the European Cup for the first time 12 years later are the glorious highlights of my career.

But meeting a man who is a giant of his generation, who has changed the world after making the incredible journey from prison cell to the presidency, is something I will cherish as long as I live.

Coming face to face with Nelson Mandela at his South African home was almost overwhelming. And what he said to me made the hairs on the back of my neck stand up.

It was in the summer of 1997 that I was asked by Littlewoods, who then sponsored the FA Cup, if I would take the trophy around the world to raise awareness of the Roy Castle Cause For Hope Appeal, launched after Roy was diagnosed with lung cancer in 1992 and, sadly, died from the disease in 1994.

Roy's widow Fiona, Liverpool Echo journalist Arthur Johnson, representatives from the charity and Littlewoods, and Professor Ray Donnelly, a cancer surgeon who founded the Foundation in Roy's name, joined me in a party of 10 for our globe-spanning trip. Under the banner World Tour Of Hope, we were away for more than three weeks.

I don't think the fact that I held the record for FA Cup appearances played any part in Littlewoods asking me to make the trip. I'm pretty sure they didn't even know that at the time – and I certainly didn't!

They invited me because I was a member of their Spot The Ball panel and it turned out to be the journey of a lifetime.

Wherever we went we were greeted not just with a welcome mat but with a red carpet. And, apart from the trip supporting a worthy cause, the magical lure of the FA Cup was evident all over the world. People of all nationalities had their picture taken with the cup. It was like a magnet.

We were wined and dined in embassies; met ambassadors, other top diplomats and politicians in the various countries; and the progress of our trip was chronicled by Arthur's reports for the Echo, Channel One Television and local radio.

We started off by flying to America, where we visited Washington DC and Los Angeles, then on to Tokyo – where the whole party sang You'll Never Walk Alone in a nightclub live down a broadcast line for local radio!

From Japan we travelled to Hong Kong. The British colony was in a state of some apprehension because Britain's 99-year lease on the territory was only weeks away from expiring and being handed over to China. Despite the obvious demands on his time, the last governor, Chris Patten, met us and made us very welcome

Nelson Mandela: I was surprised to learn that he's a Liverpool fan!

before we flew on to Sydney, Australia.

After that it was on to Dubai before we touched down in Cape Town. Obviously we hoped to be able to meet Nelson Mandela, who had become president of a post-apartheid, fully democratic South Africa in 1994, four years after he had emerged from 27 years of incarceration in jail.

But to arrange a meeting with the great man was easier said than done. Eventually, after intense discussions with the authorities and politicians, we finally arrived outside his house.

It was all cloak and dagger. Armed security men were thick on the ground but, suddenly, out onto the veranda to greet us – the FA Cup in its special box – came Mandela: a huge man, standing around six feet two, with a tremendous presence. He had an incredible aura.

I was towards the back of our party but Arthur ushered me forward and said: "Mr President... may I introduce you to former Liverpool player Ian Callaghan."

Mandela moved towards me, shook my hand and said: "I don't think I should ever wash my hand again."

I was flabbergasted. You don't get better than that! And I was further surprised to learn that he was a Liverpool fan and had kept in touch with the club's games and results by listening to the radio during his lifetime behind bars.

That meeting with Mandela was still dominating my thoughts for the final leg of our world tour, back in Europe in Brussels, before our return home.

A year later, the foundation set up in Roy's name opened the International Roy Castle Lung Cancer Research Centre, the first of its kind in the world dedicated to researching the disease. The £16 million centre, in Liverpool's London Road, was officially opened by Sir Cliff Richard.

To help raise funds for the ground-breaking centre I was involved in arranging a match at Anfield between members of the 1966 World Cup squad and Everton and Liverpool players.

I feel privileged to have played a small part in supporting the charity, and indebted to Littlewoods for giving me the opportunity to meet Nelson Mandela.

This father of the bootroom was no ordinary Joe

Bill Shankly and Bob Paisley have their rightful places in the pantheon of great managers, but another member of Anfield's "football brains trust" is all too often overlooked, even at times airbrushed out of the game's history.

Joe Fagan was a special kind of guy and what he didn't know about football would fit on the back of a postage stamp.

So when Manchester United won a treble in 1999, with the plaudits quite correctly showered on Sir Alex Ferguson, I immediately recalled the first time an English club won three major prizes in one season, 15 years earlier.

It was Liverpool under Joe's command who stormed to the league title, European Cup and League Cup in 1983/84 in his first season after succeeding Bob as manager.

Given the plush millionaire lifestyle of managers and players today, it's incredible to reflect that while Joe's team were tearing up football's record books he continued to live with his family in a modest terraced house just a few goal-kicks away from Anfield.

But that was Joe. No airs or graces, as down to earth as they come and a man without any pretensions. But don't make the mistake of thinking he was ordinary. Far from it.

Joe's wisdom about the game was phenomenal and he didn't suffer fools gladly. He was a lovely man and I have only fond memories of him.

I remember once during Bill Shankly's time as manager when I had a race to be fit for a home game. We were staying at the Lord Daresbury hotel pre-match, but I came back to Anfield with Joe for treatment.

Before we got to the ground, Joe invited me to his house for a spot of lunch. His wife Lil made me some scrambled eggs and after that we went to Anfield where Joe gave me some treatment and got me fit to play.

Could you see anything like that happening today in the Premier League? Certainly not. More likely you'd have a team of medics and dieticians hovering around you.

Tommy Smith tells an honest story of how, having just signed professional forms, he refused to sweep the dressing room when he was asked by one of the coaching staff.

Then a voice behind him said: "Pick up that brush and do as you're told." It was Joe and it was typical of him. You just didn't argue with him.

He was a great football man who always got his point across and made a massive contribution to Liverpool's success even before he took over the manager's seat.

I think he's unique, too, for the fact that he worked for both Harry Catterick and Bill Shankly. Before Harry joined Sheffield

Wednesday prior to becoming Everton manager, he was boss at Rochdale where Joe was trainer. Harry recommended him to Liverpool and he arrived at Anfield in May 1958.

It was Joe and Bob who set up what became a football institution, a place of myth and legend... the famous Anfield bootroom.

Its origins were quite humble. Joe and Bob used to coach and treat players from the Guinness Export team, and as a thank you their manager Paul Orr, later a Lord Mayor of Liverpool, sent some crates of the black brew to Anfield.

The question of where to keep them was answered when they were stacked in the room where the boots were stored.

When Bob, Joe, Reuben Bennett and others on the backroom staff fancied a drink after a day's training or after a match, they would go into the room, sit on a crate or on a skip basket and chew over the topics of the day. That's how the legend was born.

Contrary to popular belief, Bill Shankly hardly ever went into the bootroom. It was the domain of his backroom team, and after matches Shanks would invariably hold court with the press in the corridor outside or go to his office.

The opposition managers and coaches would be invited into the bootroom and given a drink, although the choice was quite narrow! When Elton John went in there on Watford's first top-flight visit to Anfield – admitting he was more nervous entering the bootroom than playing a massive New York concert – he was asked by Joe what he'd like to drink.

"Could I have a pink gin, please?" asked the superstar.

"Sorry, lad," said Joe. "You can have a Guinness, a brown ale or a Scotch. That's yer lot!"

I also used to be invited in on occasions after my long-time pal Roy Evans had joined the coaching staff.

Me with Joe in 1977. He deserves more credit for what he achieved

I took it as a great privilege, but one I certainly didn't abuse.

I was still playing, so if a manager came in I would politely say my goodbyes and leave. I remember being there when Brian Clough came in after a match, but I didn't hang around for a chat.

Quite apart from anything else, it was a small, cramped room and there wasn't much space. There weren't any windows either.

But thanks to Joe and Bob the vision that shone from within those gloomy, enclosed walls put Liverpool's name in lights. It's just a great pity that Joe's name often lacks the illumination his deeds so richly deserve.

We all had the same golf handicap: Bill Shankly!

Bill Shankly believed that if you played football you trained for football – and nothing else. He scoffed at clubs who sent their players road running or scaling sandhills. "We play on grass so we train on grass," he insisted.

That is why golf was on his list of what not to do for players. He told us that after a morning's training he didn't want us "traipsing round a golf course in the afternoon", as he put it.

He used to say that by using different muscles you could get a strain or a pull. So we were very much discouraged from getting out the bag of clubs.

But having said that, Shanks used to go to watch the Open when it was at Royal Birkdale. His favourite player was the great Australian links expert Peter Thomson, who won the Open five times including twice at Birkdale and once at Royal Liverpool.

When Thomson won his fifth title in 1965 at Birkdale, Shanks walked round in the gallery watching him do it. So it wasn't that he didn't like golf.

He just didn't want his footballers to play it.

I didn't really take up the game until I'd hung up my boots. Roger Hunt and Tommy Lawrence, though, were keen golfers and tried to sneak in a few rounds. But Shanks was soon on the case.

When he found out he rang the secretary of Leigh Golf Club and told him that Roger and Tommy weren't allowed to play!

My route into golf came through Geoff Strong when I went into the pub and restaurant business with him when I finished playing. Geoff already had a successful upholstery company and we took over the Golden Lion at Rainford and the Hesketh Arms at Rufford.

Geoff was a very keen golfer and a member at Hillside. I took lessons and eventually I joined Hillside, too. Over the years the game's brought me great enjoyment as well as many of those moments when you're sure the ball's going to drop and it doesn't!

My spot prize really started something

I took only two penalties in my entire career in competitive football: the first at the invitation of the rest of the team and the second because it was my turn and I had little choice in the matter.

Many people seem surprised that despite playing almost 1,000 games I didn't take more.

Well, it's just that I never considered myself as a penalty taker and I'm in good company because some of the great strikers – Kenny Dalglish and Ian Rush are prime examples – either didn't take penalties or took them only occasionally.

There is an art to penalty taking which has little to do with the position you fill. There is undoubtedly a big mental factor involved: the ability to close your mind to everything else as you step up to the spot – what that great penalty exponent Jan Molby calls "going to another place".

And that can apply equally to great attacking players such as Billy Liddell, who had thunder in his boots, or Phil Neal, a full-back who was an expert at directing the ball past the goalkeeper from 12 yards.

It just wasn't for me. Yet, the first penalty I took was almost forgotten – thank goodness! – in the jubilation of Liverpool clinching their first league title for 17 years.

The date was Saturday, 18 April 1964 and we kicked off against Arsenal at Anfield knowing that if we won we'd be champions with three games to spare and we'd be bringing the crown back to the Kop for the first time since 1947.

The atmosphere was one of the most expectant I have ever experienced at Anfield. The boss, Bill Shankly, went on radio at lunchtime and told supporters that if they didn't leave for the ground early they wouldn't get in.

He was right. The gates were closed an hour before kick-off and Roger Hunt had great difficulty getting through the crowds to have a pre-match fitness test. But he made it on both counts.

The crowd went wild when we took the lead after only seven minutes, Ian St John taking a pass from Alf Arrowsmith and sliding a shot past goalkeeper Jim Furnell, our former team-mate who had left us to join Arsenal in a £15,000 move the previous November.

But despite our best efforts we couldn't break through again before Arsenal had a great chance to dampen the premature celebrations on the half-hour when our skipper Ron Yeats handled a George Eastham flick.

George took it himself but Tommy Lawrence showed what a fine keeper he was by diving to his right and turning the ball for a corner. I was soon to know exactly how George felt!

By half-time we'd scored again, through Alf Arrowsmith, and two Peter Thompson goals and one by Roger put us 5-0 up after an hour and sent the fans wild.

We thought we'd made it six a few minutes later when Alf had

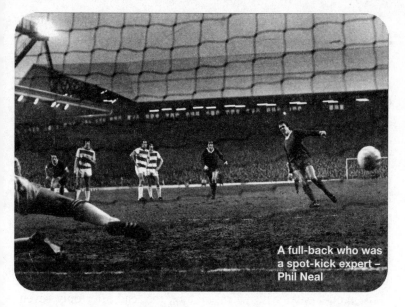

A full-back who was a spot-kick expert – Phil Neal

the ball in the net again but the referee had already blown for a penalty for a handling offence.

It was quickly decided by the rest of the lads that as the other four of the five forwards had already scored – don't forget this was still the era of the 2-3-5 formation – they would give me the chance to complete the set by taking the penalty.

Who was I to argue?! I stepped up, sent my kick low but Jim Furnell literally fell on the ball on the line to keep it out. Fortunately, the save didn't cost us. We coasted to the final whistle on a wave of joy, knowing that the title was ours.

The scenes at the end were unbelievable as the supporters who had lived through those dismal days in the old Second Division rapturously celebrated the club becoming champions... and as we did a lap of honour my saved penalty was forgotten.

By the time I took another I'd almost forgotten it myself. It was more than a decade later when I next put the ball on the spot. The date was 10 August 1974 and the occasion was the Charity Shield against Leeds, the first time the curtain-raising fixture was staged at Wembley.

We were still coming to terms with Bill Shankly's decision to retire, announced to a stunned nation only a month earlier, and the appointment of Bob Paisley as his successor.

Shanks led us out at Wembley and the game was largely forgettable. Phil Boersma gave us the lead in the first half and Trevor Cherry equalised 20 minutes from the end.

But the afternoon will be remembered for Kevin Keegan and Billy Bremner swapping punches and being sent off by referee Bob Matthewson. As Kevin trooped off he threw his shirt to the ground. Both Kevin and Billy ended up with unprecedented 11-match bans.

So it was against this bad-tempered backcloth that the game ended in a draw which meant a penalty shoot-out.

Alec Lindsay, Emlyn Hughes, Brian Hall, Tommy Smith and Peter Cormack were all spot on with our opening five penalties – but so were Leeds.

Leeds goalkeeper David Harvey was next up. But he blazed his kick over Ray Clemence's bar. I was next in the order, with the destination of the Shield at my feet.

David, having missed his attempt, took guard in the Leeds goal and I felt quite calm. I hit it well and, I'm delighted to say, sent him the wrong way as the ball hit the net to his right.

That was the sum total of my penalty experience, apart from a lighthearted episode in my 1977 testimonial match when referee Kevin McNally let me take me a penalty three times until I managed to beat Alex Stepney, who was in goal for the Lancashire

Select that drew 2-2 with Liverpool.

But when I hit the deciding penalty against Leeds at Wembley in 1974 I had no idea what I was starting. It was Liverpool's first penalty shoot-out and the outcome set the pattern for decades to come.

Over the course of the following 33 years Liverpool were involved in 11 penalty shoot-outs in domestic and European competitions and rivalled the German national team for spot-kick efficiency.

Liverpool lost only one of those 11 – in the League Cup at Wimbledon during Graeme Souness's management era in December 1993.

But there is little doubt about the club's most famous spot-kick triumph, before Istanbul. It has to be that wonderful climax to the 1984 European Cup final against Roma in their own Olympic Stadium when Joe Fagan's side emerged victorious after the wobbly legs cameo by Bruce Grobbelaar and deciding penalty by 1981 match-winner Alan Kennedy.

I'm delighted that what I began at Wembley became a wonderful Liverpool habit!

Seeing red over the divers

If someone had mentioned diving when I was playing in the 1960s and '70s, my immediate response would have been to visualise someone in a wetsuit and a face mask about to plunge beneath the waves, or a competitor preparing to spring from a high board into a swimming pool.

It would certainly not have conjured visions in my mind of a footballer throwing himself to the turf in a cheap and cheating attempt to win a penalty or free-kick.

The antics of Francis Lee – or "Lee Won Pen" as he became known – were so eccentric and rare that he was the exception that proved English football's unwritten rule in that era, namely that professionals didn't dive, notwithstanding the fierce tackling and mud-heap or ice-bound pitches that were the norm in those days.

Diving was something we encountered when we went into Europe – especially with Italian teams – and it prompted a great sense of relief that our game was not cursed by it.

Then the Premier League was formed, the barriers came down, foreign players poured into our game and in little more than a decade the whole culture changed.

During the 1990s when Roy Evans was Liverpool manager, he warned that Drury Lane would be coming to a football stadium near you any time soon; that the "imports" would dive as part of a gamesmanship that was par for the course on the continent.

His prophecy came true in spectacular style with Ronaldo, during his Manchester United days, hitting the ground with a regularity that made Francis Lee seem permanently upright!

Diving is now endemic in English football and, frankly, it sickens me. I have never believed in "win at all costs", and I have to say that even one or two Liverpool players have been infected by the diving disease.

Referees and their assistants, having to make instant decisions in the blink of an eye, cannot be expected to spot the transgressors.

Peter Walton and his fellow officials, for instance, were totally hoodwinked by David Ngog in Liverpool's home game against Birmingham in November 2009, the referee awarding a penalty for a supposed foul by Lee Carsley when it appeared that there had been no contact.

So my solution to end diving in English football would be twofold: give the guilty player an automatic red card (their manager would soon spread the message!) and install the so-called "eye in the sky" off-pitch technology so that a quick look at the film would reveal whether a player dived or not.

Cricket has introduced a new review system and there's no reason why football should not follow suit, especially when the watching media at Premier League games can see almost instant replays on their TV monitors in the press and radio boxes. It is ridiculous that the media can check things when the officials are denied.

Neal or Lawler?

Back to picking my all-time best Liverpool XI, and on to the subject of right-backs.

My choice has to be between Chris Lawler and Phil Neal, both outstanding players and both with the priceless knack of putting the ball in the net, although Phil's total of 60 goals was mainly due to his penalty-taking expertise as I've already touched on.

Chris scored 61, all from open play, which is a record for a full-back in the top flight of English football. While I was an amateur when Bill Shankly arrived as manager in 1959, Chris was on the club's ground staff.

He started as a centre-half and, after Shanks signed Ron Yeats, Chris asked for a transfer in the belief that his path to the first team was blocked. Shanks told Chris to leave it with him but I haven't the slightest doubt that he wouldn't have entertained losing him.

Instead, he switched Chris to right-back where his elegant style was crowned with his wonderful ability to "ghost" into space, bringing a different dimension to full-back play and scoring crucial goals, as well as winning England recognition.

Phil Neal's expertise at penalty taking was remarkable. On

paper, beating a keeper from 12 yards might seem easy. But put that into match conditions with a baying crowd and nervous tension, and the task becomes transformed.

But as Phil demonstrated by scoring from penalties in two European Cup finals – 1977 and 1984, and in the latter he also scored from open play – he had a perfect, ice-cool temperament.

You don't amass 23 winner's medals with Liverpool and collect 50 England caps as Phil did without being an extremely talented defender, and his £60,000 arrival from Fourth Division Northampton as Bob Paisley's first signing in October 1974 was a triumph for the club's scouting system.

Chief scout Geoff Twentyman had watched Phil several times and seen him play in a variety of positions, noting in his log after one performance: "Done well all round. Good prospect."

Geoff's observations were sufficient for Bob to pluck Phil from obscurity and plunge him into a potentially awesome debut in a Mersey derby at Goodison owing to an injury pile-up.

Phil walked from his digs across Stanley Park with his boots in a brown paper bag to launch what would become a glittering career spanning 11 years and 650 Liverpool appearances, and he gets the vote at right-back in my team, just ahead of Chris Lawler.

Secret French boots, shinnies and the 'Tomlinson T!'

Fernando Torres, Steven Gerrard and the rest of today's stars can wear a new pair of boots every week if they so wish because they are made specially to fit their feet. I used to keep mine for the entire season and take them to the cobbler's for repair!

It took so long to break in a new pair that a groundstaff lad called Stevie Marshall, who took the same size as me, used to wear my boots to break them in and I used to pay him for doing it.

And right through my career I used to take my boots to the cobbler's shop on Priory Road, close to the ground, to get them patched up if they'd been ripped.

Although at school I played in the heavy, old-fashioned type of boot, with the reinforced toe cap and straps, when I started my professional career I wore the lightweight, streamlined Continental boots and I made sure I looked after them. There's no way I could give away my boots for after-dinner fund-raising auctions as many of today's players do because it took too long to break in new ones.

We also had a secret weapon in our armoury in the form of a set of French-made, weather-beating boots that enabled you to keep your feet in icy conditions when other teams would be slipping and sliding all over the place!

They had ridged soles and I think the club had only one set of them. The company that made them ceased production so that when players left the club they weren't allowed to take those boots with them. They were handed down.

The club had that set for years and we'd wear them home and abroad if conditions demanded. One classic example of their value was in deepest Poland during Bob Paisley's reign as manager in November 1975. The temperature was minus 10 at kick-off in our UEFA Cup third-round first-leg meeting with Slask Wroclaw.

The pitch was just a sheet of ice yet, armed with our magic boots, we kept our feet while the Poles struggled. We won the game 2-1 through goals from Ray Kennedy and John Toshack, and went on to lift the trophy that season by beating Bruges in the two-leg final.

Now, of course, we wouldn't need that type of boots because all top clubs today have undersoil heating and, in general, Premier League players don't have to contend with icy pitches.

Whether we wore shin pads was optional and I had a spell without them. I felt so much better even though I took the chance that I might have got a nasty kick.

If someone raked the front of your shins with his studs you'd know about it! But, other than a few cuts and grazes, I got away with it. So I was fortunate.

Whereas today the Premier League decide on a designated ball, as part of a commercial deal, clubs used to choose their own.

Shanks chose the type of ball we played with at Liverpool. It was called the "Tomlinson T". It was orange and a fantastic ball, and I think we were fortunate that Shanks made that decision because it was great to play with.

When you kicked it, the ball's flight was true. It might not have suited today's free-kick experts, though, who have developed their art thanks to new technology in the manufacture of balls which enables them to bend and swerve in the air.

As for kit, I think fashion dictates trends. When I first started watching Liverpool, the players wore long shorts. Then in the early 1960s came the briefer versions, and now longer shorts are back in vogue.

Replica kit has become an amazing money-spinner for clubs, giving them huge financial incentives to introduce new styles and colour combinations every season. Football has become an integral part of the fashion industry.

However, you can't help but have sympathy for low-income families who try to keep up with it all because youngsters always want the latest styles which are far from inexpensive.

Anfield's James Bond? Pictured with Ron Yeats at a sports dinner

Hello, Mr Bond
I presume...

Imagine relaxing by a Spanish pool on holiday when you are suddenly joined by James Bond!

It happened to my late wife Lin and I when we were staying as guests of Jimmy Tarbuck at his place in Marbella.

The story began when we met the racing driver James Hunt on our flight to Spain. Jimmy knew him and had asked James to say hello to us on the plane, which he did. He came to our seats, introduced himself and we later went to a couple of restaurants in his company.

But one day Jimmy and his wife Pauline went off to play golf, leaving Lin and I on our own by his pool. Then we heard the sound of a gate opening and suddenly there in front of us was Sean Connery, James Bond himself. 007 in the flesh.

Lin and I looked at each other somewhat shocked and, I suppose, speechless. It was mind boggling. Here was probably the most recognisable man in the world standing in front of us and we were tongue-tied.

Then, in those rich, resonant tones in which he addressed so many villains and so many beautiful women in those ground-breaking movies, he said to us: "Hello, is Jimmy about?"

"No, sorry," I said. "He's gone golfing with Pauline. I'm Ian, this is my wife Lin and we're Jimmy's guests."

"Well, will you tell him I called, please," said 007.

"Certainly will," I said. "No problem."

Jimmy had organised a golf match with himself and Sean Connery playing Peter Lorimer and Norman Hunter, who had flown out with the rest of the Leeds United team for a summer break.

So on the day of the golf match Jimmy said to me: "Come on, we'll go down to Sean's house." Well, it was just unbelievable. And that's when I was properly introduced to James Bond.

We then went to the golf course where we were joined by Michael Parkinson, who also had a place nearby and who I already knew.

I wasn't into golf in those days, so Parky and I walked around to watch the game. They played for a few bob and the Leeds lads won. Sean wasn't too pleased with the turn of events and at one stage broke his putter in sheer frustration.

Even James Bond couldn't get the ball down the hole as quickly as he hoped!

13

The day Shanks's flash car caused a big stir in the neighbourhood

The question of who was the greater – Bill Shankly or Bob Paisley – has been asked with increased frequency over the years, even prompting a vox-pop question to supporters as a regular feature in the club's match programme.

Yet for me the answer is simple. It has to be Shanks, because without him goodness knows what the future of Liverpool FC would have been, and Bob would almost certainly never have become manager and embarked on his incredible haul of 19 trophies in nine seasons.

I think Bill Shankly is the greatest figure in the entire history of the club. For me, he's the best thing that's ever happened to Liverpool FC. Bill is the greatest motivator I have ever played for and Bob the greatest tactician, but when Shanks arrived in December 1959 he was the first manager ever to pick the team, a factor which had led him to turn down the job seven years earlier when the directors selected the side.

The state of the club – both physically in the dilapidated condition of the stadium and in Liverpool's stature, marooned in the old Second Division – was at such a low ebb when Shanks took over that it's hard for today's younger supporters to appreciate.

Shankly rightly described Anfield as a slum. He knew that the training ground at Melwood – and the training methods – were far from satisfactory and, clearly, the players were nowhere near good enough to lead Liverpool back into the top flight, especially with a £12,000 ceiling placed by the board on transfer signings.

But Shanks, the outrageous extrovert, grabbed hold of the club by the scruff of the neck. He retained the entire backroom staff, got rid of 24 players and persuaded the directors that investment in new talent had to be increased.

He was fortunate in the latter quest in that John Moores, the great Everton beneficiary whose family also had interests in Liverpool, arranged for his Littlewoods financial wizard Eric Sawyer to join the Anfield board as financial director.

Mr Sawyer gave Shanks unstinting boardroom support and told him: "Mr Shankly, if you find the players, I'll find the money." And that's exactly what happened.

Shanks rebuilt the club on and off the field, and when it came to the end of the 1960/61 season, with Liverpool having missed promotion yet again following their relegation in 1954, Mr Sawyer's backing proved crucial.

Motherwell wanted £37,500 for Ian St John and one director stood up at a board meeting and said: "We can't afford to sign him." Mr Sawyer responded: "Gentlemen, we can't afford NOT to sign him."

So Shanks got his man, Ian scored a hat-trick on his debut against my much-missed friend Brian Labone in a Liverpool

Shanks:
Like a
second
father to
me

Senior Cup game at Everton, and after Ron Yeats followed Ian to Anfield later that summer we were on the march back to the top flight of English football.

I have my own gratitude to Shanks because after watching me play as an amateur in the junior teams at Melwood and then in the reserves at Anfield he asked me to turn professional.

My mum and dad were very wary of me taking such a step because I was an apprentice central heating engineer and, therefore, had a reasonably good trade in prospect. Without that, if I didn't make it in football I'd be on the scrapheap.

I told Shanks that I'd love to turn pro but I couldn't say yes or no until he'd had a chat with my parents. The arrival of Shanks in his Ford Corsair, which he parked outside our Toxteth tenement block in Caryl Gardens, was a big event in the neighbourhood.

My mum made him a cup of tea and Shanks told her and my dad that he wanted me to sign pro. He told them that he'd keep me well fed and look after me – and he was as good as his word. For 14 years he kept me under his wing and shaped a large part of my life. He was like a second father to me and I never had a fall-out with him – there was never a wrong word between us and I never had to ask for a pay rise!

The relationship I had with him was never better illustrated than after our European Cup Winners' Cup victory over Standard Liege in Belgium in December 1965.

We'd already won the first leg at Anfield 3-1, through a couple of goals from Chris Lawler and another from Peter Thompson, and after we came out on top 2-1 in the return, with Roger Hunt and Ian St John on the mark, Shanks told us we could go out to a casino quite close to the hotel.

We were playing Newcastle away on the Saturday and Shanks gave us a curfew time but Ian St John, Ronnie Yeats, Gerry Byrne and I overshot it. Not by very much – but as we got back to the hotel some of the lads shouted down from the window that Shanks and Bob were waiting for us at the door.

As we ran in, Shanks said to Ian, Ronnie and Gerry: "I told you what time to be in... I'll speak to you in the morning!" Then he saw me. He didn't say anything to me at first, but as I ran up the stairs he shouted after me: "I'm going to tell your mother on you!" I don't know about the other three but I never heard any more about it. Shanks didn't really like confrontation. Once he'd put his point of view I don't think he'd prolong it. And he'd never hold a grudge if you did have an argument with him. He'd invite you for a cup of tea. That was his olive branch.

Any row was soon all over and forgotten, and I can never recall him fining a single player for being late or for any other misdemeanour.

43 years? What's that between friends and the sweet FA?

Saturday, 30 July 1966 and Wednesday, 10 June 2009 might appear to be random dates with no connection. Yet they loom large in my life. The first was the golden day when, as a 24-year-old, I watched my England colleagues carry the World Cup around Wembley after that unforgettable 4-2 extra-time win over West Germany – a triumph I had contributed to by playing in the group win over France and setting up one of Roger Hunt's two goals.

The second date, a lifetime later, was when I received a medal to commemorate my part in England's greatest feat. It was presented to me – and to others who had waited so long for such recognition – by Prime Minister Gordon Brown at 10 Downing Street.

It was the conclusion of a tortuous campaign for the other 11 members of Sir Alf Ramsey's World Cup squad to receive official recognition – for being a part of the success and acting as back-ups to the lads who played in the final and, quite rightly, received their medals on the day.

The entire chapter does no credit to the Football Association who, after years of pressure to have the extra medals minted, finally agreed. But even after writing to inform us of their decision, they kept us waiting and wondering if and when it would ever happen.

In fact my close pal and former Liverpool team-mate Gerry Byrne, who was also in the 22, used to pounce on Brian Barwick – then FA chief executive – whenever he came to Anfield to ask him what was happening.

"Hey, Brian, when are we getting our medals?" Gerry would ask. It probably wasn't Brian's responsibility but we were all just frustrated and at a loss to know what the situation was.

And it wasn't just about getting a medal. Over the years the other 11 had been left out of things by the FA. For example, the whole World Cup squad with Alf and the coaches went out onto the balcony of London's Royal Garden Hotel after we'd come back from Wembley with the trophy. We were all thrilled to bits as we waved to the crowds. It was one of the great moments in our sporting history.

Yet, years later, when it came to staging an anniversary re-construction of the balcony scene back at the hotel, just seven members of the team were involved.

Again, when the new Wembley opened it was only the lads who'd played in the final who were invited. The rest, including myself and Gerry, were neglected.

Even the late Sir Alf, the only England manager to win the World Cup, never received a medal, and I understand he paid himself to have one struck! That, to me, is a scandalous reflection on the FA, who should have ensured Alf's unique achievement was afforded a suitable accolade.

Worth the wait: Pictured with my solid gold World Cup medal

Instead, they acted far too late because when we got our medals at Downing Street, right-back George Cohen received a belated medal for Alf on behalf of his widow. There were also medals for the families of the late Harold Shepherdson, Alf's assistant, and trainer Les Cocker. At least the FA realised their debt to Sir Alf by erecting a bust of him at Wembley, which was unveiled by his successor Fabio Capello.

The public campaign for medals for the "other 11" began after a

Sunday People column by Mike Langley appeared some 15 years ago. Langley said that it was shameful to have ignored the team behind the team, including three of us – myself and fellow wingers Terry Paine and John Connelly – who had appeared in the finals.

It was later taken up by the Mail On Sunday, and in 2005 FIFA president Sepp Blatter announced that they would take action, and also for all other members of previous World Cup-winning squads. But it took another four years before we had the medals in our hands, a far cry from the situation when Italy won the 2006 World Cup and were presented with 45 medals... for all 23 of their squad and 22 for the coaching and backroom staff.

I know our captain Bobby Moore wanted us to get official recognition because it had been planned for the £22,000 due to the squad to be paid proportionately.

But Bobby insisted to Sir Alf that the money be split equally through the squad. So thanks to him each of us collected £1,000. I think Bobby had a lot to do, as well, with the Inland Revenue's decision to waive tax on our prize money.

The other members of the "shadow" 11 in addition to Gerry Byrne, Terry Paine, John Connelly and myself were Peter Bonetti, Ron Springett, Jimmy Armfield, Norman Hunter, Ron Flowers, George Eastham and Jimmy Greaves.

I have to admit that after playing well in our 2-0 win over France in our final group game, and crossing the ball for Roger Hunt to head one of his two goals, I half expected to stay in the team for the next game, which was the quarter-final against Argentina.

Alf had left Alan Ball out of our last two group games against Mexico and France when he played wingers. So I was quite surprised when Alan came back in, Geoff Hurst was selected and Jimmy Greaves and I dropped out.

But Alf saw his route to glory with his so-called "wingless wonders" and you can't criticise him for that, even though the repercussion of it was a dearth of wingers in English football. Thankfully for Peter Thompson and myself, Bill Shankly had no intention of taking Alf's tactical route.

Alan Ball repaid Alf's faith brilliantly. He was phenomenal, a great player who gave us all kinds of problems at Liverpool after his £110,000 British record move from Blackpool to Everton a couple of weeks after the World Cup.

On the day of the final, in that pre-substitute era, I had a special task... looking after Nobby Stiles's false teeth! He gave them to me in an envelope before kick-off but said to me: "If we win the cup, Cally, for goodness sake get my teeth back to me at the end so I've got them in for the photos."

I sat in the stand behind the Wembley band box, with the rest of the non-playing members of the squad, and when the final whistle went the celebrations were amazing and I just couldn't get to Nobby to give him his dentures.

That's why he's famous for the picture of him dancing with joy on the Wembley pitch with that big, gap-toothed smile. So, in a way, I did him a favour.

Little did I know then that myself and 10 other members of the squad would get so long in the tooth waiting for our medals.

Treading the boards is much scarier than crossing that white line

Playing football in front of crowds of up to 100,000 is something I could handle without nerves gnawing away inside me. As I walked onto the pitch I felt the adrenalin running but certainly not my stomach churning. It is what I did. It was the job I was trained to do.

But walking out on stage at a packed theatre is very different. And recently that's exactly what I've done. It's been a new and challenging experience.

In 2009 I was invited by John Keith, producer and writer of The Bill Shankly Story stage show and my collaborator on this book, to join the cast of the long-running production as stand-in for Ian St John at New Brighton Floral Pavilion.

I was delighted to accept the invitation although I did so with a mixture of eager anticipation and no little apprehension. We played to a full house that night and it was a wonderful atmosphere – but so very different from playing football.

Showman: At my testimonial show with Patsy Ann Scott

When I played I felt in command of the situation. But walking out on stage that sense of control isn't there. It reminded me of the nerves I've felt standing on the first tee in a celebrity golf tournament when your name is announced because, essentially, it's not your thing.

But joining The Bill Shankly Story meant that I linked up again with my 1960s and '70s team-mates Chris Lawler and Ron Yeats in recalling the memories and anecdotes of the Shankly years live on stage.

Chris is a revelation in the show. As a player he was a man of few words but now he takes the microphone on stage like an old-fashioned comedian and relates some terrific Shankly stories, while Ian St John and big Ron have always been highly accomplished talking to audiences. John Keith speaks Shankly's words in the show and Steve Hazlehurst, who brilliantly plays the title role in The Dixie Dean Story, narrates.

My next job in the Shankly production was to stand in for big Ron, when illness forced him out of a corporate lunch version of the show at a city-centre hotel, after which I was invited to join the cast on a permanent basis.

That's when the nerves really hit because we did the show at the Liverpool Empire on Monday, 14 December 2009, exactly 50 years since the Monday in 1959 when Shanks arrived at Anfield for his first day in charge.

I had been on stage at the Empire back in February 1978 to take a bow at the end of my testimonial show, which was a fabulous evening. My old mate Jimmy Tarbuck organised the show and topped a bill which also included Michael Parkinson, the late, great Dickie Henderson and the reigning Miss World, Mary Ann Stavin – later squired by Graeme Souness and George Best.

But to be a part of the show myself in the Shankly production was very different. With a near full house of around 2,000 people in that incredibly impressive theatre that night, with the atmosphere electric, the butterflies really started to flutter, I can tell you!

Having said all that, it was a great pleasure to be a part of it and to stand there at the end to tumultuous applause. To know the audience enjoyed it so much gives you such a buzz.

The show premiered in September 2006 and has been staged to packed houses throughout Merseyside as well as in Norway and Ireland.

The fact that it's still going strong, with more bookings in 2010, reflects not only the quality of the show but the seemingly everlasting appeal of Bill Shankly.

(For details of performances of The Bill Shankly Story, email thebillshanklystory@hotmail.com, or write to: PO Box 518, Southport PR9 9WN)

Oh, what a night
– with Smithy in
Rome, 1977

Silk and steel

I have one immediate choice when coming to select the centre-backs in my Liverpool XI: Alan Hansen. If Chris Lawler fashioned a new style of full-back play, then Alan did the same at centre-back.

He just oozed talent, and the greatest compliment I can pay him is to say that he was a similar player to Bobby Moore and Franz Beckenbauer. Like those two gentlemen, Alan always seemed to have time on the ball. He was magic to watch and had skills that many midfielders would die for.

I wonder whether any manager at any time has ever signed three better players than Bob Paisley did when he landed his "Treble Scotch" of Alan, Kenny Dalglish and Graeme Souness.

Alan cost only £100,000 from Partick Thistle, which was an incredible bargain given his subsequent feats for Liverpool over 13 years and 630 appearances: captaining the club, appearing in eight title-winning teams and playing in the European Cup final wins in 1978, 1981 and 1984, amongst a cascade of other honours.

When he hung up his boots, Alan simply transferred his laid-back, languid style of playing to a laid-back, languid style of broadcasting which has made him football's number one television pundit.

Having installed Alan as one of my centre-backs, one of the most difficult jobs was deciding who should partner him because there's a list of superb candidates... Ron Yeats, Emlyn Hughes, Phil Thompson, Mark Lawrenson, Sami Hyypia and Jamie Carragher amongst them.

But I've opted for my old room-mate and team-mate at both Liverpool and Swansea, Tommy Smith. I'm choosing him not for any sentimental reason but for the fact that he would be a perfect foil for Alan Hansen.

Smithy's gritty, combative attitude is an essential in any team. He didn't know the meaning of the word fear, and he was living proof that when the going gets tough, the tough get going.

Unremitting in the tackle as he was, that shouldn't fool anyone into thinking he was all muscle. Smithy personified fighting spirit but he was also a fine player; a great passer and distributor.

Bill Shankly said of Smithy that "he was born a man, he was never a boy", and that captured his qualities. Regardless of how well or otherwise he was playing, Tommy would always gee up the rest of us and for that reason I would have him captain my side.

The smell of coffee and the scent of success

They say that smell is one of the most powerful and evocative of all the senses and whenever that wonderful aroma of fresh coffee hits my nostrils I am transported back to the very early 1960s.

Jimmy Tarbuck, Bobby Campbell and I were the coffee-bar kids, and our regular venue was the Kardomah in Church Street, right next to the long-gone Tatler news and cartoon theatre.

Tarbie was then an up-and-coming comedian who had a meteoric rise to the top, while Bobby was a Liverpool team-mate of mine, a wing-half who later managed Fulham and Chelsea.

All three of us were Scousers, and Jimmy and Bobby were great pals. So after training each day I'd go down to town to meet up with them, have a laugh and get through several cups of coffee.

The Kardomah was the in-place then, even though it didn't sell alcohol and drugs weren't even on the radar. Everyone seemed to gravitate there, including many of the singers and musicians who created the phenomenon of the Mersey Sound.

As soon as you reached the door, that rich smell of coffee beans hit you. We'd sit round the table and exchange stories, and Jimmy would entertain us with tales from his job as a Butlins holiday camp redcoat.

It's amazing to think that just a few years later he was on television's big show Sunday Night at the London Palladium and, almost overnight, nationally famous.

Jimmy's been a mate of mine ever since, and he's been a life-long Liverpool fan. He's rightly proud of the fact that he's one of the very few people Bill Shankly allowed into the dressing room before games to crack a few gags – Shanks believed that laughter was a good way of helping you loosen up.

But if you'd lost, he didn't like people laughing. He revealed that he once heard one of his Preston team-mates laughing in the dressing room after they'd been beaten, and he told him: "You should be out in jail for that!" Typical Shanks.

Jimmy's father Freddie was a bookie and an Evertonian, and Jimmy tells the story of how his dad and some of his pals took him as a youngster to a Mersey derby at Goodison.

They were all shouting for Everton but when Liverpool scored Jimmy threw his hands in the air and cheered, drawing gasps from his dad and his mates, with one of them exclaiming: "Bloody hell... the kid's a Red!" He wasn't wrong!

My pal Labby: much missed and never forgotten

I played against Brian Labone in many Mersey derbies but, apart from shaking hands at the end and exchanging a few words, we never really knew each other.

It was only after we'd both hung up our boots that we formed a close friendship and when I came to realise what a great guy Labby was.

His sudden and shocking death in April 2006 left a gap that can never be filled because Labby was unique. That word is too often bandied about, but in Brian's case the description was precise. When he left us they broke the mould.

He was a charming, unforgettable big man, often irritating and often argumentative, but his heart was always in the right place and if you had Labby as a friend he was unwavering in that friendship. In fact, if he had a fault it was that he couldn't say no to people.

They would ask him to do this, do that, go here, go there and, invariably, he would agree. He was going out night after night to

Golf day: My pal Brian Labone was always helping people out

attend functions and I used to say to him: "Labby why do you need to do all this? You've done your share over the years. Take some time out."

But he still took so much on himself and the problem was that he was so disorganised. He didn't have a diary. He used to write dates of functions and events on the back of his cheque book.

Then, when he'd used all his cheques, he'd inadvertently throw away the cover! So he never knew where he was supposed to be turning up.

I got to know him when I joined the Littlewoods Spot The Ball panel. When Joe Mercer stepped down I took over his place on the panel, of which Brian was already a member.

Later, I moved to live in Lydiate, near to Brian's home, and that's when we became really friendly. I used to pick him up on Saturday mornings to go to the Spot The Ball office and later drop him off at Goodison where he was a greeter on match days, proudly wearing his smart Everton blazer.

We'd regularly have a pint at our local The Weld Blundell – or "The Welly" as it's known – and then he got me onto the after-dinner circuit, mainly with another great Evertonian, former goalkeeper Gordon West, doing question-and-answer sessions.

I was a pall-bearer at Labby's funeral in Liverpool Cathedral and I've never seen a funeral like it in my life for the number of people who came to mourn the passing of one of Merseyside's greatest sons.

It's good to know that Brian's widow, Pat, is keeping the family's Goodison connection going by taking on the role of secretary of the Everton Former Players' Foundation. He would be delighted about that.

Labby, the player his manager Harry Catterick called "the last of the Corinthians" was a superb centre-half and captain of Everton, for whom he made 534 first-team appearances and was booked only twice. He also won 26 England caps.

It was a privilege to have played against him and a privilege to have him as a friend. Labby, rest in peace.

My Istanbul half-time team talk was just as hard as Rafa's

I have never seen a more incredible mood swing amongst well-heeled corporate diners than I witnessed at Anfield on the evening of Wednesday, 25 May 2005 thanks to the amazing events on the other side of Europe at Istanbul's Ataturk Stadium.

My job on that unforgettable night in Liverpool history was to join Ronnie Moran and compere John Keith to speak at the club's official European Cup final dinner in Anfield's Champions Suite, where the game was beamed live on several large screens strategically placed around the function room.

The hundreds of diners came from all over the UK... and one man, in particular, symbolised the almost unbelievable shift of fortunes on the field in Turkey as Liverpool collided with AC Milan to decide the destination of European football's greatest club prize.

When I arrived for the dinner, ready to say a few words and watch the game, the mood was distinctly upbeat.

Everyone seemed optimistic that Rafael Benitez could end his first season as managerial successor to Gerard Houllier by bringing the magnificent trophy back to the Kop for the first time since Joe Fagan's side toppled Roma in their own Olympic Stadium in 1984.

I was excited, quite naturally, not only as a life-long Liverpool fan but also by the wonderful memories the occasion invoked of being a member of Bob Paisley's team that won the club's first European Cup by beating Borussia Moenchengladbach 3-1 – also in Rome – in 1977.

During that heady period when the club went on to win the great prize four times in seven years, a special bond developed between Liverpool and the European Cup, or "Old Big Ears" as Phil Thompson so affectionately called it.

Now we were gathering over dinner hoping to re-acquaint ourselves with our old, glittering friend after an absence of more than two decades.

Little did we know what a mental roller-coaster lay in store for us or that the final would become the first game to span two days with the last, dramatic, nerve-jangling, gut-wrenching acts of an epic contest being played out at almost one o'clock in the morning, local Turkish time.

Over the course of the season, starting at the third qualifying round stage, Liverpool had seen off the challenges of Grazer, Monaco, Olympiakos, Deportivo La Coruna, Bayer Leverkusen, Juventus and Chelsea to secure their place in the final against Carlo Ancelotti's fancied Milan.

Alas, the sound of Spanish referee Manuel Gonzalez's whistle to commence battle had hardly faded when that richly experienced European campaigner Paolo Maldini put the Italian club ahead...

and the bubbling atmosphere in the room began to lose some of its fizz.

And by half-time, after Hernan Crespo had added further goals, it had become chillingly and depressingly flat. Ronnie, John and I had to get on our feet and speak during the interval, and while we all thought Liverpool's mission was now no more than a damage limitation exercise, the three of us agreed that we would try to be positive rather than deepen the gloom.

That was when I spotted him... a Leicester businessman and fervent Liverpool fan slumped over his expensively booked table, not through an over-consumption of wine but in tearful and utter dejection at the 0-3 scoreline.

That image captured the mood of the whole room, and as the second half began Ronnie, John and I wondered what on earth we were going to say to the audience at the end of the game.

In reply to John's questions, the first point I made was that we were lucky only to be 3-0 down. The way the first half had gone Milan could easily have had five.

I also said that the manager was almost bound to make a change of some kind for the second half and that I didn't believe Liverpool could play as badly after the interval as they had before it.

I told the audience that if we scored soon after the break then anything could happen.

I suppose that all those observations were being echoed in Benitez's half-time dressing room team talk when he would also remind the players that the supporters were still backing them to the hilt.

Then, nine minutes after the restart, Steven Gerrard scored. Suddenly there was a ray of hope. Two minutes later, Vladimir Smicer added another Liverpool goal and the glum, tearful atmosphere around the tables had made way for smiles of expectation.

Perhaps that Smicer goal revealed that the football gods were not only smiling on Rafael Benitez and his players but also writing the script – a script that would have been summarily dismissed if it had been presented as a believable work of fiction.

Benitez had raised a few eyebrows by including Harry Kewell in his starting line-up even though the Australian had been struggling during the season with a groin problem and had been taken off in the final league game against Aston Villa 10 days before Istanbul.

He lasted only 23 minutes against Milan before the gamble failed and he was replaced by Smicer. The Czech Republic midfielder had become accustomed to the sight of the substitute board, or as my team-mate Terry McDermott called it, "the toast popper".

This was the 74th time he had been sent on – more even that "super sub" himself, David Fairclough, who was sent on from the bench on 62 occasions – and he had been taken off in 76 games.

But he will be remembered for his contribution in Istanbul, which turned out to be his farewell Liverpool appearance before his summer departure on a free transfer to Bordeaux, later re-joining his first club Sparta Prague before taking charge of the Czech national team.

And when Xabi Alonso completed a three-goal Liverpool salvo in a five-minute span, Mission Impossible now looked highly achievable.

By now our Anfield suite was jumping and when Jerzy Dudek produced his stunning double save from Andriy Shevchenko I

thought the roof was going to lift.

By the time the game went into a penalty shoot-out our emotions had been stretched and hung out to dry! What more could this amazing occasion produce?

The answer was a defiant act of goalkeeping by Dudek: told by Jamie Carragher to follow Bruce Grobbelaar's off-putting line movement in Rome in 1984, the Polish keeper saw Serginho slice the opening spot-kick high and wide.

Dietmar Hamann, another substitute (who had replaced Steve Finnan after 45 minutes), drilled in his penalty before Andrea Pirlo was denied by Dudek diving to his right.

Liverpool made it 2-0 on penalties when Djibril Cisse sent Milan keeper Dida the wrong way with a side-foot shot before Jon

Dahl Tomasson did the same to Dudek.

John Arne Riise's kick was saved by Dida to his right, and when Kaka scored in Dudek's right corner the shoot-out was tied at 2-2.

Time for Smicer to take centre stage again, and when he coolly found the net he became the first player to score European Cup final goals on successive days... his in-play strike coming on 25 May and his penalty on 26 May, local time.

And when Dudek saved Shevchenko's penalty Liverpool had won the European Cup in a manner that will never be repeated, with pundits and public alike struggling to find the superlatives to do it justice.

Ronnie, John Keith and I picked up our microphones in an attempt to hail the incredible achievement we had just witnessed, but as a seemingly never-ending conga of jubilant supporters snaked past us we realised we had better give it up.

And our man from Leicester, who had been in the depths of despair at half-time? He was asked politely if he would stop dancing on the table.

The letter that bridged more than 11 years

Eleven years is longer than the span of many players' entire careers. For me it was the length of time that passed between my second England cap and my third... an English record of 11 years and 49 days, to be precise!

We were playing at Middlesbrough in our opening league game of the 1977/78 season, a match in which Kenny Dalglish celebrated his league debut for us with a seventh-minute goal to earn us a 1-1 draw.

Before the game, Ronnie Moran told the lads that the new England manager Ron Greenwood wanted to have a chat to a few of us. As I hadn't played for England since the World Cup finals group game against France in July 1966, I said to Ronnie: "Well, one thing's for sure... he won't want to talk to me." And, quite honestly, I didn't think any more about it.

So you can imagine my shock a few days later when a letter dropped on my hall mat informing me I had been included in the squad for Ron's first game in charge – a friendly against

Switzerland at Wembley.

I was one of seven members of the Liverpool team that had won the European Cup in Rome four months earlier to be called up by Ron, although Kevin Keegan had since moved to Hamburg.

The others were Ray Clemence, Phil Neal, Terry McDermott, Emlyn Hughes and Ray Kennedy, and we all felt a bit sad that Jimmy Case wasn't with us as well.

But that was Ron's decision. He said that he wanted to harness our club understanding at international level and, good enough, he picked all seven of us in the team.

That night Switzerland played above themselves. We just couldn't fashion a breakthrough and the game ended goalless. It was frustrating, although I was delighted with the comment in Mike Payne's book, England: The Complete Post-War Record, which states:

> *"England's best and most attractive movements invariably began at the feet of the evergreen Ian Callaghan. Recalled to the side for the first time since 1966, he used all his experience, and his delightful passing deserved better support from his colleagues.*
>
> *"One long ball from him almost brought about a fortunate goal when Hasler, thinking wrongly that he was under pressure, almost put through his own goal. But Burgener dived to save."*

I stayed in the side for our next game, the World Cup qualifier in Luxembourg the following month, when goals were the order of the day to boost English hopes of reaching the following summer's finals in Argentina which, ultimately, proved fruitless.

My England career didn't pan out exactly as I expected

We managed only a 2-0 win in the Grand Duchy but at least I set up both goals with crosses for Ray Kennedy and Paul Mariner.

That was the end of my resurrected England career. But at the age of 35, it had been beyond my wildest dreams to be recalled in the first place and I'll always be grateful to Ron Greenwood for earning me a place in the record books.

Callaghan to have operation

10 OCT 1970

Ian Callaghan, Liverpool's 27-year-old forward is to have a cartilage operation next week.

The mystery knee injury that has kept him out of the game for three weeks was finally diagnosed yesterday as cartilage trouble—and confirmed pool's worst fears.

Since Callaghan, the club's senior professional with more than 450 appearances behind him got a knock on the knee against Nottingham Forest, he has had treatment and training.

But the injury has failed to respond properly and fears which have grown steadily that it would finally turn out to be a cartilage were confirmed yesterday.

Callaghan will go into hospital next week and will be out for several more weeks.

This is a considerable blow to Liverpool. They already have Bobby Graham out of the game at least until Christmas with a broken ankle.

Windham bowls

... Monday's

Ian Callaghan

800 not out for the ageless Ian!

Eight hundred not out! Ian Callaghan, the marvel of Anfield, makes his appearance today ...

★ Michael Charters — on Callaghan, the man and his record.

I trust the Anfield spectators will make Cally's day something special ...

Cally's 800th senior appearance is not a Football League record as the following statistics show, but he is well in line to establish it ...

Tommy Paine (Southampton and Hereford)—805

Roy Sproson (Port Vale) Cup 10.

Jimmy Dickinson (Portsmouth)—815 appear-

off your week

You need a bit of luck to be a marathon man

Bill Shankly once likened me in a radio interview to a rubber ball. "Whenever Ian goes down on the field he bounces straight back up again," Shanks declared.

Well, a "bounceability" quality is not all you need to string together hundreds of appearances as I was able to do for Liverpool along with other marathon men such as Phil Neal, Emlyn Hughes, Tommy Smith, Jamie Carragher and Steven Gerrard.

Obviously you need to perform well enough to keep being selected by the manager. You also need a massive slice of good fortune to avoid being ruled out by injury, because a long run in the team does wonders for your confidence.

Conversely, the longer you're out of the team the more your confidence is eroded.

I had only two major injury problems in my Anfield career. The first was a cartilage operation in 1970 and the second was an Achilles problem in 1977.

The first one was deeply worrying for me. Cartilage surgery

then was a long-term affair, your absence measured in weeks or months rather than the days it takes to recover from today's keyhole surgery techniques.

I had real fears that, at 28, my career could be over. I injured my knee before the season started but after treatment it seemed to clear up.

Sometimes a dislodged cartilage, which is a piece of gristle between the joints, can pop back into place and then come out again.

This must have happened to me because although I played in the opening nine games of the season, a cartilage problem was diagnosed in September.

I had the operation done in a Manchester nursing home. It was the first time I'd been in hospital and I was worried stiff and apprehensive about my future.

I was out of the game for three months, and during my absence we saw the emergence of university graduates Steve Heighway, a flying winger, and Brian Hall, who could operate down the flank or inside.

When I returned to first-team action in the Fairs Cup game at Hibs in Christmas week, I found the going hard. After five league games I found myself out of the team again.

I gritted my teeth and got back in again in March and played in the FA Cup final against Arsenal two months later when we lost 2-1 after extra-time.

But the cartilage surgery opened up a whole new chapter of my career. I was switched from being a raiding winger to a central midfield position, essentially operating in front of the back four in the role that Javier Mascherano fills today.

The demands of the midfield game were not totally strange to me because I'd been a half-back as a youngster and I wasn't averse to going into a tackle.

When Kevin Keegan had arrived from Scunthorpe for £35,000 from Scunthorpe in Cup Final week, he'd been signed by Shanks as a midfield player, which might have put the squeeze on me!

But Kevin's attacking display in a practice match at Melwood just before the start of the following season persuaded Shanks to pitch him in up front alongside John Toshack in our opening League game against Nottingham Forest.

Kevin scored after 12 minutes – and the rest, as they say, is history. I missed that first game when John McLaughlin got the nod. But I was back for our next match against Wolves wearing the No 11 jersey for the first time. It heralded a new lease of life for my career because I had that number for the next seven years.

My Achilles problem flared up in March 1977 in our famous European Cup quarter-final second leg against St Etienne, won so dramatically by super sub David Fairclough.

I was out for the next 12 games of our bid for an unprecedented treble, which included a stint on the bench as an unused substitute for our FA Cup semi-final replay win over Everton.

It was May before I tasted action again, as a 61st-minute substitute for David Fairclough at Queens Park Rangers, but I was a spectator again as the lads secured the league title with a goalless home draw against West Ham.

Then the boss, Bob Paisley, had a 13 into 11 dilemma when he sat down to choose his line-up for the FA Cup final against Manchester United, the second leg of our treble attempt.

David Fairclough missed out completely and I was named as our only permitted substitute, eventually replacing David Johnson for the last 27 minutes of our disappointing 2-1 defeat.

Walking off the Wembley pitch I felt miserable. Not only had we lost and seen our treble chance disappear but I feared I'd miss out again on a place for our European Cup final against Borussia Moenchengladbach, which was looming the following Wednesday in Rome.

But in training on Monday, Bob came over to me and said: "Would you like to play in Rome?" He knew the answer before I blurted out: "Yes!"

In the Eternal City all my fitness problems and worries about getting back in the team evaporated in the joy of helping Liverpool lift the European Cup for the first time.

What do they say? No pain, no gain!

It's left to a local hero

I have three contenders for the left-back position in my all-time best Liverpool XI team: Gerry Byrne, Alec Lindsay and Alan Kennedy, all of them England internationals and all quite different types of player.

Alec, it was claimed, arrived by accident from Bury for £67,000 in March 1969. The story goes that it was a case of mistaken identity because Shankly thought he'd signed another player entirely!

It's said that the realisation happened on the training ground one day when Shanks said to Alec that he'd like to see him score some of the goals he'd frequently knocked in for Bury.

"Not me, boss," Alec is said to have replied in his broad Lancashire brogue. "You must be thinking of someone else." Alec had played as a wing-half and inside-forward for his home town team but was hardly a prolific scorer.

According to the story, the man Shankly thought he'd signed was Alec's Bury team-mate Jimmy Kerr, who scored 38 goals for the

Tribute to a hero: Me at Gerry Byrne's testimonial – on a snowy night at Anfield in 1970

Shakers from midfield.

I didn't witness the reported incident at Melwood and Alec swears it's not true, describing the tale as " a load of nonsense" and adding: "Don't tell me Shanks wouldn't have known who he was signing. It must have been one of his jokes."

What is beyond contradiction is that Alec became a first-class left-back for Liverpool. He was a member of the league title and UEFA Cup double-winning side in 1972/73, and of the 1974 FA Cup-winning team.

His unflappable defensive style earned him a call-up by caretaker England manager Joe Mercer – who was a fine judge of football flesh – to play four times for his country in 1974 and never finish on the losing side.

A year after Alec left for Stoke he was followed into Anfield by

Alan Kennedy in August 1978. The £330,000 Alan cost from Newcastle was then a record fee for a left-back but, like full-back partner Phil Neal, his Anfield career carried a hallmark of European Cup glory.

His only goal of the 1981 final against Real Madrid in Paris, scored from a tight angle, is written into Liverpool folklore, and so is his winning penalty in the shoot-out against Roma in their own Olympic Stadium three years later.

But Alan also had great pace and tackling ability, and he and Terry McDermott had both impressed for Newcastle against us in the 1974 FA Cup final even though they were on the losing side.

One curious aspect of Bob Paisley's signing of Alan is that, as a boy, Bob used to buy fish and chips from a shop in County Durham where he was served by Alan's mother. Sadly, she didn't live long enough to see Alan join Liverpool... but she would have been proud of what he achieved.

Strong though the claims of Alec and Alan are for the left-back berth in my team, I have to give it to Gerry Byrne. He was a superb two-footed player, equally comfortable using his left or right, and earlier in his career did appear at right-back for Liverpool.

He was a local boy who came through the ranks at Anfield. He signed as an amateur as a 15-year-old in 1953, and when Bill Shankly arrived more than six years later he was on the transfer list.

Shanks immediately removed his name because he knew Gerry could play. In fact, he possessed all the qualities Shanks looked for in a player.

He was skilful, brave, hard as nails but strictly fair.

Gerry's raw courage was demonstrated in an incredible manner in the 1965 FA Cup final against Leeds. His collarbone was shattered by a sixth-minute challenge by Bobby Collins yet Gerry continued playing through the remainder of the match and the entire half-hour of extra-time without Leeds having an inkling of his injury.

As if that wasn't enough, he provided the cross for Roger Hunt to score the opening goal in our 2-1 win. It was an amazing display of bravery by Gerry, and no wonder Shanks said: "Gerry should get all the medals himself."

That day at Wembley we were also given an insight into Bob Paisley's expertise at injury diagnosis. Bob knew as soon as he examined Gerry out on the pitch that his collarbone was badly broken yet the Wembley doctor disputed it, saying there was no break. Perhaps he just couldn't believe that a player with a broken collarbone could do what Gerry had just done. And he wouldn't be alone in that!

On the train journey back to Liverpool with the cup the next day, the story of Gerry's heroics was public knowledge. So many fans kept asking how he was that we wrote out a notice and stuck it on the inside of our compartment window, reading:

Gerry's had treatment and he's comfortable

So the back four in my all-time best Liverpool XI, with the required blend of skill and steel, reads: Phil Neal, Alan Hansen, Tommy Smith, Gerry Byrne.

Second Best!

First it was George Best.

And then me. Yes, I followed in Besty's gifted footsteps as only the second English player to have my own fan club.

During the 1960s, the Liverpool match programme ran a feature asking supporters to vote for their favourite player, and the upshot was that Linda Poole, then a 15-year-old who lived in Huyton, set up an Ian Callaghan Fan Club.

I got a bit of leg-pulling from the lads but I was very flattered. Linda was a lovely person who worked very hard at organising the fan club and I got to know her mum and dad.

She devoted a lot of her time to the project, sending out photographs and mailing newsletters. She took it very seriously and I helped in any way I could with pictures, news and gossip from Anfield.

It ran for quite some time and gave me an insight and appreciation into how fan clubs work and how demanding it must be for people who run them for major stars.

Shanks used to rehearse his famous ad-libs

My abiding memory of Shanks before games was of him coming in and out of the dressing room and going to the sink for plastic cups of water, which he'd continually sip. He was oozing nervous energy. He'd walk up and down with his hands in his raincoat pockets, chatting to the players. Then he'd comb his hair while looking into the mirror.

The trainer Albert Shelley, who'd be busy doing all the pre-match jobs, would be Bill's target for testing out his views, opinions and one-liners to see what reaction he got before he'd deliver them to us, the players, or even later to the media.

Shanks would do the same with the backroom staff such as Bob Paisley and Joe Fagan on the way to training. If they laughed or agreed, he'd deliver the particular line later for public consumption.

In the dressing room before games, Albert would just agree with whatever Shanks came out with, and say: "You're right, boss." So, in effect, Shanks was doing what many top comedians do... rehearsing his ad-libs!

For a man of no great education he had a great vocabulary. He was fantastic with words and how he used, selected and fashioned them into unforgettable phrases. His timing was wonderful and he had a way about him that made you sit up and listen. He could have been a stand-up comedian.

What many people overlook is the fact that under Shanks we didn't land a trophy between winning the Charity Shield at Everton in August 1966 and doing the league and FA Cup double in 1973.

We qualified for Europe every season during that period – and also lost after extra-time to Arsenal in the 1971 FA Cup final – but the lesson Bob Paisley revealed that he had learned from those barren years was that you simply cannot afford to be over-loyal to players.

The break-up point didn't come until we got knocked out of the FA Cup by lowly Watford in February 1970. It was only after that that Shanks began to build his second great team, and by the 1971 Cup final, Ray Clemence, Alec Lindsay, Steve Heighway, John Toshack, Brian Hall and Alun Evans had come in and an unknown called Kevin Keegan had just signed.

If ever we lost twice on the run it was a full-blown crisis in Bill's eyes and he'd have us in the office one by one. I'm not a goodie-goodie – and I don't pretend to be one – but when I was called in to see Shanks he'd say to me:

"We had to call you in – but just carry on as you are. And if we tell you to go through the motions in training, just go through the motions. Don't overdo it." I enjoyed training so much they must have thought I was doing too much!

Once, Shanks even said to me: "Do you want to talk to me about any of the players not pulling their weight? Have you got any complaints against anyone?" I said: "No. Not at all. Everything's fine."

We still don't know the full reasons for Bill's amazing decision to walk away from Liverpool in the summer of 1974 and I think he must have regretted it.

I don't know what he thought he was going to do because he could never have settled for anything outside football, which was his life. It was his drug. Perhaps he thought he would be given an input into the club at some kind of director level which, of course, never happened.

He was quite hurt and bitter about that but I suppose you can also understand Liverpool's point that they wanted to avoid a repeat of the Manchester United situation where Matt Busby joined the board and overshadowed his managerial successors by his very presence.

Bill was a stickler for fitness and I've always wondered whether the situation he found himself in, cut off from club football, contributed to his shock, untimely death at only 68.

Day Tony Bennett came to watch the Reds – and I became a fan

Anthony Dominick Benedetto – Tony Bennett to you and me – first came into my life when I was a member of the Liverpool squad that toured America in the summer of 1964.

Two years earlier, a song that had lain almost forgotten about in a drawer was rediscovered and recorded by Tony and became not only his signature tune – ironically for a New Yorker – but also an enduring standard.

I Left My Heart In San Francisco was all the rage when Liverpool arrived in the States, and it really introduced me to his music.

At that time I was into The Beatles, The Rolling Stones and other sounds of the '60s, and I hadn't become aware of Tony Bennett, even though he'd had number one hits with ballads such as Because Of You, Cold Cold Heart and Rags To Riches.

But his eulogy to San Francisco – a city we visited on tour –

made a big impression on me and I became a big Bennett fan, especially as he made the progression from Italian-American ballad singer to a full-blown jazz performer and went on to capture a whole new generation by wowing them at Glastonbury.

A decade after our trip to America, Tony was playing the Liverpool Empire and, through our chief executive Peter Robinson's friendship with the theatre manager, my close pal and business associate Geoff Strong and our wives Betty and Lin were fortunate enough to get tickets to see him.

Geoff had retired from playing by then but I turned out for Liverpool at Anfield in the afternoon only to discover after the match that Tony Bennett had been to see the game.

Peter told him that Geoff and I and our wives were going to his show that night, and when we arrived at the Empire we were taken to the dressing room to meet the man Frank Sinatra (no less) acclaimed as "the singer's singer".

For some reason the wives didn't come with us to meet him, and there we were just the four of us in the star's dressing room: Geoff Strong, Tony Bennett, his manager and yours truly.

We asked him if he'd enjoyed the game and he said he had, although I'm not sure how much he understood about our football. Geoff and I told Tony how much we loved his music and he couldn't have been more charming.

Considering he was about to go out and perform, he was so relaxed. What a great guy! And what a fantastic singer!

He went out on stage and he was just superb. It was a truly memorable night.

Team-mates, room-mates and Shanks's steaks

The thought of Tommy Smith literally breathing down your neck is one to bring fear into the minds of opponents. But, for me, it was a comforting experience and one I went through for years, spanning hundreds of games.

When we left the dressing room for the start of the game, Tommy and I would be near the front of the line and he would always be right behind me. As we reached the top of the tunnel ready to take to the pitch he would give my neck and shoulders a gentle rub.

That was our pre-match ritual and, given the success we were both privileged to enjoy at Liverpool, it's one I look back on with reassuring memories.

And after Bob Paisley succeeded Bill Shankly as manager, Tommy and I would also have a nip of Scotch just before we went out. Bob had a bottle in the medical bag and made it available to us.

I think it was something that Bob and his generation used to do when they were players. In fact, Bob recalled as a young footballer in County Durham being given sherry and eggs before schoolboy games.

Some people might mock superstitions and pre-match routines but they are important to the individual concerned. No two players prepare for a match in the same way, and anything that gets you in the right mindset is surely to be welcomed.

My routine never changed. As soon as we arrived at the ground on the coach from our pre-match hotel, I would leave complimentary tickets on the door for family and friends then head straight to the dressing room and stay there until the bell went to go out onto the pitch.

I used to take my time getting ready, starting with putting my shorts on, then my socks and then my boots. My shirt was the last thing I put on although I didn't lace up my boots until we were about to go out.

Other players were different. Kevin Keegan, for example, being the livewire he was on and off the field, used to buzz around all over the place as he never had a care in the world. You almost wondered if he realised there was a game on!

He would dart in and out of the dressing room, and Bill Shankly would often ask where he was. Then he'd be back, get changed quickly and be ready to play just minutes before we went out, whereas I'd be ready at least an hour before.

Another thing I liked to have was a pre-match rub down, usually from Reuben Bennett although Bob and Joe Fagan would also do the massages.

During my Liverpool career I had three room-mates.

My first one was Gerry Byrne – who I have just chosen as my best Liverpool left-back. He was a great influence on me and is still a very good friend of mine to this day.

I don't know how it came about, but Gerry roomed with me from when I broke into the team regularly in 1961 until he hung up his boots eight years later because of a knee injury.

Gerry had a similar background to me. Both of us were born into Catholic families in Liverpool, we both played for Liverpool Schoolboys and both came through the ranks at Anfield, although it needed the sharp judgement of Bill Shankly to prevent Gerry from leaving the club.

After he'd retired as manager, Shanks chose Gerry as his most memorable player in a conversation with my collaborator on this book, John Keith. He couldn't have made a better choice.

I remember getting back to the Grosvenor House hotel on Park Lane with Gerry after the 1965 FA Cup final, when he had played with a broken collarbone. His performance that day was one of football's greatest acts of heroism. Gerry's arm was in a sling and I had to help him get changed and put his jacket on before going downstairs to the first FA Cup-winning reception in Liverpool's history.

I watched the whole of that 1965 final against Leeds again for an LFC TV show recently, and I still don't know how Gerry managed to play all the way through to the end of extra-time. He was just tremendous, going into tackles with his injured arm by his side when he must have been in great pain.

Gerry was one of the few players who was equally good with either foot. Left or right he was terrific, and he played in both full-back berths, winning two England caps. He was a true two-footed player, and he and I were both in Sir Alf Ramsey's 1966 World Cup-winning squad.

He still has trouble with his collarbone now, a legacy of his Wembley courage, and because of that and the knee problem that forced him to reire from the game, he had to give up his job as a joiner at Pontins Holiday Camp in Prestatyn because it affected his mobility.

Being a room-mate of Gerry's really rubbed off on me, especially his fashion sense, because he was always immaculately dressed.

When we went on a summer tour of America in 1964, Gerry had the new-style drip-dry shirts which he'd wash at night, put on a hanger and they'd be ready to wear again in the morning.

That was the start of our life-long friendship and he comes through to Liverpool regularly from his home in North Wales and we go out for a spot of lunch.

I also roomed with Alec Lindsay. He was a quiet guy who bred pigs during his early careeer at his hometown club Bury, and since he retired from the game in 1983 he's been a scrap metal merchant, a pub licensee, a fish and chip shop owner and a gamekeeper, and the last I heard of him he was living in Scotland.

As I mentioned earlier in this book, there was a famous story that when Bill Shankly signed Alec from Bury for £67,000 in March 1969, he got the wrong man! Liverpool throught they'd signed a goalscoring midfielder. But that was actually Jimmy Kerr!

As it turned out, Alec was a superb acquisition as a left-back. He had one of the best left foots I've ever seen at Liverpool.

He was deservedly called up to play for England during Joe Mercer's memorable period as caretaker manager in 1974, and was never on the losing side in his four international appearances.

My third room-mate was Tommy Smith who, of course, is one of the club's greatest characters and one of football's true hard men, as indeed was Gerry Byrne.

But, like Gerry, Tommy was a fantastic player with skill to complement his rugged approach, and as a room-mate he was a great organiser of whatever we needed.

When you had Tommy looking after you, you didn't go wanting for much! And after Liverpool we roomed together for Swansea when we played there for John Toshack.

The huge changes in football from my playing days to now are reflected even down to the way the shirts are arranged in the Anfield dressing room.

Whereas when I played you stripped next to whoever you wanted, now the shirts are arranged on the pegs in team formation: goalkeeper, defenders, midfielders and forwards.

And at half-time we always had a drink of tea. There was a tray with cups and a big pot of tea in the dressing room, although Shanks would constantly sip water from a plastic cup. Whether that was nervous tension, I don't know.

After the game he would be in the dressing room for a short time, reflect on the rest of the results that day and then go out to hold court with the press in the corridor, a far cry from the stage-managed media conferences of today.

He was in his element talking to journalists, and he'd go out to talk to them armed with a few carefully prepared lines which he'd deliver as if they were spontaneous.

While this was going on, the visiting manager and coaches would be entertained to a drink in the bootroom by Bob Paisley, Joe Fagan, Reuben Bennett and Ronnie Moran.

Views on players' diet have also changed dramatically. Shanks was so keen on us eating steaks that we'd have one before every game as a pre-match meal.

Shanks:
Give them
steak...

Chicken was the alternative, and on Fridays, myself, Jimmy Melia and Gerry Byrne, as Catholics, used to eat fish. But steak was the staple diet and Shanks used to swear by it.

His belief in giving players steak was something he brought with him from his playing days at Preston, where so much of his management and training creed was shaped and influenced.

He even asked Bob Paisley to arrange for a local butcher to deliver steak through the summer to the family home of a young midfield player called John McLaughlin, to build him up.

One day John went to the manager's office and when Shanks saw him he told him he was delighted at how well he looked. Then John asked for some time off because he and his girlfriend had learned they were expecting a happy event.

Shanks left his desk, went to the door and shouted down the corridor: "Bob, Joe come quick... we've reared a bloody monster!"

Players eating steak is frowned on now. When you talk to dieticians today they say that steak is the last thing you should eat. They are great exponents of pasta, boiled chicken or scrambled eggs.

But eating steaks as our pre-match meal didn't do us any harm. Indeed, given the huge success Liverpool had I think it did us a lot of good. You can't say it was wrong.

Sometimes, when we went to a dodgy place in Europe during the early days of the club's continental trips, we were served up some strange dishes.

Some of the soups, for instance, were just coloured water and it led the club eventually to appoint food tasters, who would travel with us and ensure that what we were given to eat was nourishing.

Two of the first to take charge of our food abroad and inspect what was being prepared in the hotel kitchens were Alan Glynn and Harry Wight, both experienced in the catering trade in Dublin and friends of Liverpool chief executive Peter Robinson.

Some places, though, were beyond the pale in the food stakes. Trabzon on the Black Sea coast of Turkey was one such outpost and Ray Clemence was the envy of us all because he'd had the foresight to taken with him several bars of Cadburys chocolate.

That was in 1976 and it was a dismal place, with several members of the party returning home with stomach complaints, although I'm told that Trabzon today shows a marked improvement.

My only hat-trick was far from the madding crowd

They say that timing in life is everything. Well, I could certainly have chosen a better match in a different situation from the one that brought me the only hat-trick of my career!

It was Tuesday, 4 December 1973, a grey, winter's afternoon in the middle of the fuel crisis and three-day week, when I hit my lone treble in our 3-1 win over Hull City in a League Cup fourth-round replay, watched by a meagre crowd of 17,120.

A picture taken by that late, great sports photographer John Dawes, which appeared in the Daily Express, perfectly captured the desolate mood of that day.

It showed me taking a corner with just two young fans watching me from behind the perimeter wall. They were the only spectators in the picture!

But while the game obviously lacked atmosphere, I was delighted to record not just my only hat-trick in professional football but my only one at any level.

For a player used to providing crosses for team-mates to score, I was on the receiving end of left-wing deliveries from Steve Heighway for my first two goals, although my opener after 12 minutes had a touch of good fortune.

Kevin Keegan was measuring up to meet Steve's cross but miscued his shot. The ball came through to me and I hit it first time from 15 yards for my first goal of the season.

My second came seven minutes later. Kevin dummied an Alan Waddle flick and I scored with a powerful shot from the edge of the box.

Alec Lindsay conceded an own goal past Ray Clemence before I completed my hat-trick in the 73rd minute from a close-range tap-in, after Steve's pulled-back centre went under goalkeeper Jeff Wealands.

I was so chuffed at scoring a hat-trick that the press lads covering the game didn't have to seek me out afterwards. I went up to the press box to talk to them!

I'm sure the media people would love Fernando Torres or Steven Gerrard to do that today instead of the managed press interviews that are part of the modern game.

One of the writers who covered the game, Denis Lowe of the Daily Telegraph, wrote in his report: "I hope I'm there on the day when Ian Callaghan gets his next hat-trick. The quiet man of Anfield deserves a crop of them... and every other honour the football gods can povide."

Well, I never did get another treble. And I've no idea why because I managed to get in a fair number of shots.

But my hat-trick was celebrated by an Evertonian, a man called Jack Phillips who, with his wife, ran the Punch Bowl pub in Sefton, which was then the local for myself and Gerry Byrne.

One of the regulars made a plaque which read: "Ian Callaghan, scorer of a hat-trick against Hull City, League Cup, December 4, 1973." He brought it to the pub, and Jack put it on the wall next to the serving hatch.

You could say it certainly had rarity value!

'Grandad' Cally whips Hull all on his own

LIVERPOOL 3, HULL CITY 1—by Horace Yates

LIVERPOOL hailed their unlikeliest hat-trick hero, Ian Callaghan, affectionately dubbed "grandad" by his team mates, as the senior member of the side, as he safely steered Shankly's men into the quarter finals of the League Cup in the fourth round replay with Hull City, yesterday. Liverpool are now away to Wolves.

It has taken Callaghan 617 games to achieve his first hat-trick, a distinction that had ceased to figure among his targets, following a debut at 17 against Bristol Rovers in 1960. No wonder, when Callaghan smashed his shots home in the fashion of a demon marksman, made such a delayed celebration appear remarkable, for few players in the club boast a more powerful drive.

The match, satisfactory as it was, with Liverpool's progress, belonged almost exclusively to Callaghan. Before the match he was reminded by Kevin Keegan. "You haven't got a goal yet, Cally." Before the end Keegan, as top scorer, was pleading with him to stop, before he took over the mantle.

"It's good practice for the 'derby' on Saturday," reminded a defeated Callaghan——to look out, Everton!

Hull manager Terry Neill, who had promised to murder Liverpool, must have feared a scoring avalanche in a first half so dominated by Liverpool that it looked more like a practice session than a cup tie.

The goal flow could have started in the fourth minute, when Keegan missed a Heighway cross in front of goal, but there was no respite in 12 minutes, when Callaghan took over.

Whether the blow would have fallen so quickly had not a generous referee allowed Cormack to take a free kick seven or eight yards from the position of the offence, is debatable.

The lively Heighway, who gave McGill a roasting all afternoon, centred and the ball came out to Callaghan just inside the penalty area. Hitting the ball perfectly, Callaghan gave the stranded Wagstaff no sort of chance.

Seven minutes later Liverpool were two up and again it was the deadly right foot of Callaghan that destroyed Hull. With Keegan and Callaghan racing towards Lindsay's cross, Keegan

24-hour news has ended a special relationship

Distance, they say, lends enchantment, but one thing I know for sure is that the relationship between top-flight football and the media was totally different – and better – during my playing career than it is today.

We didn't even call it the "media". The sportswriters were known as the "press lads" and we were on friendly, first-name terms with them.

It was based on trust. We realised they had a job to do and also that if we didn't play well they would rightly criticise us. But if we told them things off the record they respected it.

The national journalists who covered Merseyside football had the home telephone numbers of not only virtually every Liverpool and Everton player but also those of the managers and coaches, too. There were no mobile phones then.

The journalists, and later local radio reporters, would turn up at Anfield or our Melwood training ground at will to interview Bill Shankly or the players.

And it was on Merseyside that pre-match press conferences with managers and players began during the late 1960s. Prior to that, the clubs would issue their team line-ups or squads through the relevant Press Association representative who would send it out on the wire to the papers.

That is not to say it was a perfect world. There were the occasional rows over something somebody had written – or a headline over their copy written by an office-based sub-editor – but generally the football people of my generation worked in reasonable harmony with the press.

To underline that is the fact that I still count among my good friends today people such as Colin Wood, Mike Ellis and my co-author John Keith. They and others travelled with Liverpool all over Europe reporting our exploits.

So why is it so drastically different today? Well, for a start the great god of money, after the coincidental advent of the Premier League and satellite television, has transformed players from sporting heroes to celebrities of pop star proportions, complete with minders, agents and public relations people.

There is now a barrier between players and the media, and with the sheer intensity of rolling 24-hour news coverage – as was amply demonstrated by the John Terry affair – I can quite understand why every club now has its own press office.

There were wars and disasters in the world, yet the Terry story was on the front page, back page and middle pages – not to mention the massive television coverage.

It has become ridiculous. When I played we used to be in the spotlight but I think today's players live in a goldfish bowl.

If a player or manager says something at 10 o'clock, it's round the world by five past! Top-flight football is now a massive business and it must be very difficult for sportswriters covering the scene today compared with my era.

But one thing's certain. As long as football remains the global game, it will continue to make headlines.

Classy Stevie, flashy Souey and the man our rivals all feared

Back to my all-time best Liverpool XI, and there are many contenders for places in midfield. They include Willie Stevenson, Gordon Milne, Emlyn Hughes, Terry McDermott, Jimmy Case, Ronnie Whelan, Jan Molby and Xabi Alonso. But none of those great players make it into my line-up.

First and foremost, and without a moment's hesitation, Steven Gerrard goes in. It's an old adage in football that every player has a weakness. But, quite honestly, if you asked me what Stevie G's weakness is I wouldn't be able to answer you.

He is the complete player. He does everything. He defends, he scores goals, he creates, he inspires, he leads. Not only does he possess the ability to dictate the course of games. He can take them by the scruff of the neck and give them a good shake, transforming a potentially negative situation into an emphatically positive one, turning possible defeat into victory.

Stevie is the game-changer supreme, an immense talent and a

fantastic product of the former youth development system that pre-dates the Liverpool Academy. He has passion, power in both feet and he's a good header of the ball.

Playing for Liverpool or England he is truly world class, and he's the type of player every Kopite would like to be and any club in the world would love to have. Liverpool can thank their lucky stars that Stevie changed his mind and turned down a move to Chelsea.

Alongside Stevie in the centre of my three-man midfield I would choose Graeme Souness – a tremendous player who carried such authority in his game and who replaced me in the team in 1978.

He was described by sportswriter David Miller as "a bear of a man with the touch of a violinist", and that captures Graeme perfectly. Armed with a powerful physique, he could bring subtlety to his play, with a great range of passing and a thunderous shot that helped bring him 56 goals in 359 Liverpool appearances.

And if the going got tough, he'd be in the thick of battle. Overriding his ability was his personality. He had a magnetism and arrogance about him which made him a great captain and prompted Bob Paisley to quip: "If you let him, Graeme would toss up with a gold-plated credit card instead of a coin."

I think Graeme will admit that his period as Liverpool manager left a lot to be desired. But his contribution on the field before his departure to Sampdoria following the 1984 European Cup win was brilliant and established him as one of Liverpool's greatest players.

On the left of midfield I'm choosing another powerful player with a wonderful touch: Ray Kennedy, the man foreign coaches feared as much as anyone. Whenever we had a European game, usually the first question posed by the opposition coach would be: "Is Ray Kennedy playing?"

Reunion: Back together again in 2007

He was such a difficult man to counter, patrolling the left flank in imperious style and then ghosting in to unleash a venomous shot. His shooting ability was a feature of his days as a front-running striker alongside John Radford in Arsenal's double-winning side of 1971 when they beat us in the FA Cup final.

Ray was signed by Liverpool chairman John Smith for a then club record £180,000 on the very day in July 1974 that Bill Shankly stunned the nation by quitting as manager. So his arrival was totally overshadowed. Yet with one of his many masterstrokes, Bill's successor Bob Paisley converted Ray from a centre-forward to a left-sided England midfielder after tracking down Ray's school teacher in Northumberland and discovering he'd played in midfield as a boy. It is a tragedy that Ray's life has been blighted by Parkinson's disease and amazing to learn that doctors now believe it first afflicted him as a teenager at Arsenal. That makes his achievements even more amazing.

Anfield: A temple of emotion

When we talk about Anfield, it immediately summons up visions of the Kop in full, raucous voice and thrilling football moments. But we must never forget that it has a deeper resonance: partly triumphant, partly sombre.

As I said, I was speaking at the club's official dinner at Anfield on the night of the Istanbul game, and when I left the ground in a taxi in the early hours I was amazed to see fans milling around the stadium and others driving around it in their cars, with horns sounding, and flags and banners tied to their vehicles.

They obviously felt that's where they should be, drawn to the stadium by some inner compulsion to pay homage to the incredible achievement they had just witnessed on their television screens.

Sadly, the same happened with disaster as well as triumph. On the weekend of the Hillsborough tragedy in 1989, I was out of the country, playing in Amsterdam as a guest for an amateur team that included employees of Hotpoint, at the invitation of my friend Jim

Donaldson who worked for the company.

But when I got home I was told how people had gathered at Anfield to lay wreaths and scarves as soon as news of the terrible events broke, and that many kept a night-long vigil.

For several weeks after the disaster, Anfield ceased to be a stadium. It became a shrine and a garden of remembrance.

I know that football must look to the future and aspire to new stadia. But we must never forget that Anfield is a temple of emotion with a permanent place in people's psyches.

Bob Paisley's 1977 regret about me

Bob Paisley, in stark contrast to the eloquence of Shanks, found it difficult to find the right words but he had a deep well of football wisdom and his powers of observation were razor sharp. And I had a similar warm relationship with Bob as I'd had with Shanks. We never had a wrong word.

When Bob – very reluctantly – took on the so-called "Mission Impossible" of succeeding Shanks after his bombshell resignation, he was determined to heed the lessons he'd learned at Bill's shoulder during their 14 years together.

One of them was to be ruthless in discarding players past their best. "Once they come down from that level it's not fair to them or the club to keep them," Bob quite readily admitted. Almost every close season he would make one big top-up signing to maintain the quality of the squad.

Tom Saunders, a man who moved from the bootroom to the boardroom at Anfield, said that he'd never known anyone who could assess a player's strengths and weaknesses quicker or better than Bob, and hailed him as a master tactician.

When you consider Bob's judgement of players, has any manager ever signed three to match his "Treble Scotch" of Alan Hansen, Graeme Souness and Kenny Dalglish?

To some people, Bob's County Durham tones were hard to understand, and the joke was that the definition of an impossible conversation was Bob trying to talk to Kenny, whose own Glaswegian tongue was unfathomable to some!

But we knew what Bob was saying and we got used to his phrases. He got his points across all right and he had a shrewd football brain. Just as I had a wonderful manager-player relationship with Shanks, exactly the same applied with Bob and I.

I cannot remember him ever shouting at me.

If he had something to say he would pull you to one side and have a quiet chat with you. Even when he left me out of the 1977 FA Cup final against Manchester United, we didn't fall out about it. I knew I was nearing the end of my career and I suppose I accepted it.

He sent me on as a substitute for the last 27 minutes, then on the Monday in training for the European Cup final two days later he ran up to me at Melwood and said: "Do you want to play in Rome?" What a question. I said: "Of course I want to play." Bob replied: "Well, you're playing."

I am eternally grateful for being a part of what happened in the Eternal City because our great win over Borussia Moenchengladbach completed an amazing journey for me... from playing in the old Second Division to collecting a European Cup medal. Fantastic!

Later, Bob told my team-mate Tommy Smith that he'd made a mistake in leaving me out of the FA Cup final. I didn't learn about that until years later but Bob was big enough to admit it and I appreciated it very much.

One of Bob's great strengths, which was invaluable to Shanks during his period as boss, was his expertise in the diagnosis and treatment of injuries.

He was a self-taught physio, thanks to a correspondence course taken when he hung up his boots in 1954 and a piece of paper signed by a close friend of Liverpool chairman TV (Tom) Williams.

The friend was the aforementioned John Moores – later knighted – and such was the clout of the Everton benefactor that when he wrote and signed a letter requesting access for Bob to visit physiotherapy units and operating theatres in Merseyside hospitals, the doors were opened to him.

His skill as a physio spread far and wide so that athletes, dancers, actors and others asked to avail themselves of his services, and on one famous occasion a woman even turned up at Anfield with a lame greyhound requesting Bob's healing hands. "I'm sorry, I don't do dogs," Bob told her apologetically.

Perhaps after the shock of Bill's sudden retirement it needed someone like Bob to take the club on to great European achievement because I think that tactically he was more sophisticated than Shanks. He had a gift in quickly weighing up opponents and employing the counters to any threats they may offer.

But he remained the most modest of men and said of his extraordinary achievements: "Bill built the house and I put the roof on it." Some house... some roof!

A week in the life...

As we all know, the life of a footballer has changed dramatically over the years. Here's an account of a typical week in my life which was written for me by Ann Cummings of the Liverpool Echo before the first game of the season in 1975. We would end the season as champions – Bob Paisley claiming his first championship as manager with that sensational and dramatic 3-1 win at Wolves in May 1976.

SATURDAY

Woke up with a morning call in our London hotel for a very special day – the first match of the season, against Queens Park Rangers. We travelled down to London last night, as usual for away matches. It's much better because you approach the game in a more relaxed frame of mind than you would if you'd had to travel the same day.

After tea and toast in bed and a look at the papers, I got up around 11am and went for a stroll round the shops with the lads to get a bit of fresh air. Then it was back to the hotel for lunch; I had my usual pre-match scrambled eggs on toast and tea.

We watched the sports programmes on television in the lounge then, and by this time the nerves were beginning to show. You always want to get the first game of the season out of the way, because you're a bit apprehensive how it's going to go, how you are going to play, after the break.

Anyway, we got the coach to the ground for about 2pm. Some of the lads went to look at the pitch, but I never bother – it's just a personal thing. I start getting ready about 2.15pm. I'm always one of the first in the dressing room, and I have a set routine – the last thing I put on, for instance, is my shirt, before I go out.

The game was disappointing, and we lost 2-0. The mood of the lads wasn't bad on the train journey back to Liverpool; we didn't play badly and a lot of good things came out of the game. It was the first one of the season, it was away from home and most of the lads were just looking forward to Tuesday's match at Anfield.

We went straight into the diner for a meal on the train and most of the lads played cards. I don't play myself; I just read the papers or a book. We were in Liverpool at around 9.30pm and after a beer in the local with some of the lads I went home to watch a bit of television before unpacking my bag and going to bed.

SUNDAY

A lovely, lazy day for me! Mind you, I don't get much chance of a lie-in for long, because our baby daughter Suzanne, who's 18 months, wakes us up early. After breakfast I went to the ground for treatment for a blister on my toe. It was a bit sore and it's as well to get it looked at right away. I took Samantha, our eldest daughter – she's five – in the car with me for a run.

The rest of the morning was taken up with typical Sunday things. I washed the car and did some gardening. Samantha helped me by picking up leaves. She's getting very helpful now and the latest thing she is proud about is that she goes to the shop to get the papers for Daddy.

After lunch my wife took the kids out for a walk while I watched Lancashire on the television. If I watch cricket it's always Lancashire and England. When the kids came in with Linda I gave her a hand to bath them and put them off to bed and then we settled down to watch the Sunday film on television.

I suppose I'm quite a telly addict – my favourite things are films, plays and documentaries.

MONDAY

It's back to work again today! I got up at 8.30am and left for the ground a bit earlier than usual so I could get my toe re-dressed. As usual we got changed at Anfield and went by coach to Melwood for the training session.

We had a team talk with Bob Paisley about Saturday's game, but we didn't do an awful lot of training because of Tuesday's match. We just did some sprints, worked on a few moves, went through things that didn't go right on Saturday and finished up with a five-a-side.

Back at Anfield I had a shower and lunch. Everyone was quite keyed up about tomorrow's game because it's the first of the season at home that everyone looks forward to. Added to that we were playing West Ham and the lads wanted to get on the winning trail before the home crowd.

I went straight home then because I was babysitting – while my wife went out. I watched the Test match on television and played with the kids, and then a man came round to look at the patio which we are having re-done. I always have an early night before a game, so I was in bed around 10pm. Before going to sleep I usually read a book for half an hour. At the moment it's Chay Blyth's The Impossible Voyage. It's a signed copy he gave me when I met him in London in the summer, which was a fabulous thing.

TUESDAY

What a day to remember! That was a cracker of a game against West Ham – and I was delighted to score our first goal in a 2-2 draw. I don't score that many (just two last season) and I get a real kick out of it, as you can imagine.

Kevin laid the ball back to me from the edge of the box and I hit it from about 18 yards to the goalie's left-hand corner, off the ground. Wasn't it an exciting game, though? West Ham are a good side and they helped make it such an entertainment for the crowds.

The day started quiet enough, because I always take it easy. Linda brought me coffee and the papers in bed, and after a lie-in I just lazed about the place. We had a decent lunch, of steak, chips and veg because I wouldn't be eating again till after the game. In the afternoon I just read – as you can gather, I'm a bookworm – and watched television.

As usual, I left tickets at the ground for my dad and brother Philip, who always go to home games, before going into the dressing room to get ready. Once I get in the dressing room, I won't come out for anybody!

By the time the referee came to check our boots I was feeling a bit nervous again – but the nerves always go once I am playing. I was probably a bit more apprehensive than normal because it was the first home game and suddenly everything was happening again for the fans and us. But it was nice to open up the account for 1975 by scoring that goal.

After a celebration drink in our players' lounge with some of my mates I was home again for a salad Linda had left for me. I didn't discuss the game with her, because I put it all behind me once I'm home. I can honestly say Linda wouldn't know whether we had won or lost by my face!

WEDNESDAY

This morning I woke up to find my thigh was pretty sore. I got a knock late on in last night's game in a tackle with Trevor Brooking, and as often happens with injuries, it had stiffened up in the night.

So it's off to the ground for treatment after breakfast. I was going to take Linda and the kids to Southport for the day to look at the zoo and the shops – but that's the way things go in football.

I had treatment at Anfield, with electric massage machines, before lunch and then another session of treatment in the afternoon. Then it was home again to play with the kids before a meal and television.

People might get the idea it's a pretty dull life. But at the start of the season, especially with mid-week games, you tend to take things easy and quiet and you don't make any appointments for a while.

THURSDAY

It's back to work for the lads again today, but more treatment for me. The thigh isn't quite so sore this morning but I have to confine my training to a walk around and a few exercises. First of all, though, I had more treatment at Anfield, supervised by Joe Fagan.

I don't know at this stage whether or not I will be playing on Saturday. That may be decided when I report to the ground tomorrow.

In the afternoon I managed to take the family out to Southport for a couple of hours. I took it easy while Linda took them round the shops for a bit of fresh air. We managed to get a babysitter for tonight so I took my wife out for a meal in the Southport area. I always enjoy having a meal out, particularly with a bottle of wine – Reisling is my favourite. But we weren't home too late so that the babysitter could get home.

FRIDAY

In at the ground at the usual time and had treatment for my leg injury before going off with the rest of the lads to Melwood. But the injury was still bad enough to keep me out of the game against Spurs and I was only able to walk around while the lads completed their training.

After lunch at the ground I had some more treatment for the injury and then went off to my mother's in Aigburth to deliver tickets for friends and neighbours.

Then it was home again for a time before going back to the ground for even more treatment. We normally go away to an hotel cn the night before almost every match of the season, so the injury meant I could have a rare Friday night at home.

I wanted to rest the injury as much as possible so I stayed in, had a snack and just put my feet up and watched television.

Special K and Shanks's hairdryer

Kevin Keegan's arrival at Anfield from Scunthorpe in the spring of 1971, when he famously sat on a bin outside the ground waiting to have transfer talks with Bill Shankly, was for me an era-changing moment.

Kevin proved not only a great player for Liverpool – much of that down to his own determined striving for self-improvement rather than dipping into a bottomless well of natural talent – but was also a trailblazer off the field.

Shanks signed Kevin apparently as a replacement for me in midfield because I'd missed much of that 1970/71 season through knee surgery, although I got back in the team towards the end and played in our FA Cup final loss to Arsenal.

But when Kevin sparkled playing up front in a practice match at Melwood just before the start of the 1971/72 season, Shanks decided to plunge him in alongside John Toshack in attack for our opening league game against Nottingham Forest.

Kevin took just 12 minutes to score, we went on to win 3-1 and a fantastic career – as well as a great partnership with Tosh – had been launched. I was happy, too, because far from being replaced I played on for another seven years at Anfield!

Kevin was as energy-packed off the field as he was on it. He was into everything. So much so that he earned the nickname "Andy McDaft".

But he was strong willed. He bought a house on top of a hill in North Wales and lived there. And despite occasionally being marooned in bad winter weather, he rejected all the club's overtures to move closer to Liverpool.

Almost as soon as Kevin secured his first-team place he became a celebrity, pop star-type personality like no other previous Liverpool player.

George Best at Manchester United was the first to achieve that status, but until Kevin arrived, players at Liverpool did their training, played the games and that was pretty much it.

Kevin soon had his own agent, made records, did TV shows, had his own national newspaper column in the Daily Express – written in conjunction with my collaborator on this book, John Keith – had courtesy cars provided by Jaguar, and ran his fan club from the back of a shop on Liverpool's Prescot Road.

By definition he was a fashion trend-setter, and the Keegan permed hairstyle swept the country. Perms were later sported by Phil Neal, Terry McDermott and Phil Thompson (pictured).

But I don't think Bill Shankly was too enamoured with hairstyles becoming a football fashion item. When the Anfield dressing rooms were being refurbished, he walked in one day, spotted a hairdryer that had been installed and created quite a rumpus.

"What's that?" he barked.

"A hairdryer, boss," one of the lads replied.

Shanks couldn't believe it.

"Hairdryers for footballers! Why the hell do you want them?" A few choice expletives followed. It was Bill's own version of the hairdryer treatment.

The European trip I would rather forget

I have travelled to most countries in Europe, and many beyond, and in the days prior to the fall of the Berlin Wall and collapse of the Iron Curtain I went to several of the former communist states.

Yet the place I have no hesitation in naming the worst I ever visited was Trabzon, on the Black Sea coast of Turkey.

The occasion was the European Cup second round first leg against Trabzonspor in October 1976, during Bob Paisley's reign as manager.

As soon as we arrived at the hotel – if that's what you could call it – Bob dashed off the team bus and went inside to check it out.

He came back, climbed on the bus and shouted: "They've put us in a doss house. We'll just have to make the best of it." He wasn't joking!

Our accommodation was quite dreadful and I still recall it in my question-and-answer sessions at sporting dinners. I was rooming with Tommy Smith and we had bunk beds. It was like a prison.

There was a hole in the floor for the toilet, the shower consisted of a bit of string which, when you pulled it, produced a few drops of water and, to crown it all, we were awakened in the early hours by chanting from the mosque right next door.

We were accompanied on the trip by hotelier Jack Ferguson, then manager of the Holiday Inn in Liverpool's Paradise Street, and he went into the kitchens to try to get us served with something nourishing.

He was fighting a losing battle, and the wisdom of Ray Clemence, in bringing with him a substantial supply of Cadbury's chocolate, was clear. Ray must have known something!

The press boys had huge problems in filing copy back to England because these were the days before mobiles and laptops.

There was one telephone in the hotel, which seemed permanently out of use, and many of the sportswriters ended up sending their match preview copy from a telex machine at a cement works, which had been hunted down by Colin Wood of the Daily Mail.

My overriding memory of the town itself was the lack of pavements. It was medieval. And when we got to the ground we were in for a shock.

The dressing rooms had mould growing on the walls, there were no windows and, suddenly, we were plunged into total blackness when the lights went out.

We just had to stand still because you couldn't see your hand in front of your face, and I'm sure the lights were switched off deliberately.

They did come back on again, but Bob went spare. And his mood wasn't helped when he saw the state of the match ball. "I played with a pig's bladder at a Durham miners' gala that was in better nick than that!" he retorted.

When we got out onto the pitch you could feel the sense of utter hostility from the tightly packed 25,000 home fans in a stadium that had a steep grass bank on one side. Perhaps not surprisingly, we lost the game 1-0, to a second-half penalty.

The whole party were just glad to get out unscathed, apart from one or two stomach upsets, and we saw off Trabzonspor with a 3-0 win in the second leg a fortnight later.

Six months after our Turkey trot we were holding the European Cup in Rome's Olympic Stadium and Trabzon seemed a long way away.

Eighteen years later Aston Villa had the honour of being drawn to play in Trabzon in the UEFA Cup and the word back was that conditions had vastly improved. They could hardly have got any worse.

If that was my worst travel experience, I suppose the place I enjoyed visiting as much as anywhere was West Germany.

Liverpool went there for many pre-season games because the hotels, the food, the pitches and the training facilities were first class.

The club had a close relationship with Gunter Bachmann, an agent who arranged the games. Gunter was a very nice guy but if there was the slightest hitch in our plans or change to our itinerary he'd get it in the neck from Bill Shankly, who was always on his guard against foreigners.

But Gunter just took it all philosophically and with a puff on his pipe because he knew that Bill's bark was far worse than his bite!

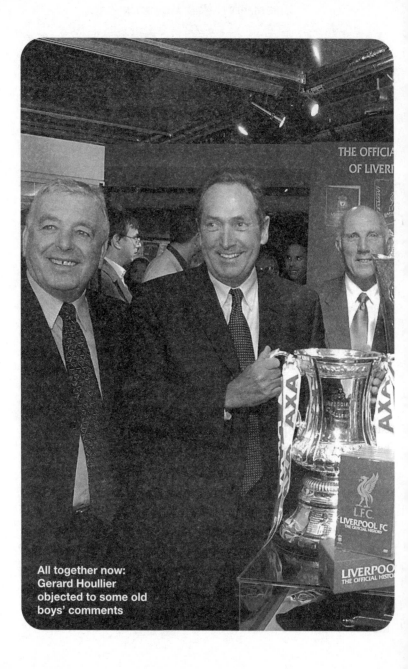

THE OFFICIA
OF LIVERF

AXA

L.F.C.
LIVERPOOL FC
THE OFFICIAL HISTORY

LIVERPOO
THE OFFICIAL HISTO

All together now:
Gerard Houllier
objected to some old
boys' comments

It's a great feeling of togetherness, old boy!

Here's a maths question you might struggle to answer:

When is 1 equal to 857?

Answer: When it comes to being eligible to join Liverpool Former Players' Association.

Our "old boy" network, which is now a dozen years old, is open to all former players who have ever kicked a ball for the club in earnest, whether they made just a single appearance or, in my case, had the privilege of wearing the jersey a record 857 times.

We set up the association 11 years ago after we'd sought the valuable advice of David Sadler, a friend of mine on the "Spot The Ball" panel who'd been involved in launching a similar organisation at Manchester United.

A few of us had mentioned that we'd like to form our own association, and it was my old mate Tommy Smith who grabbed the idea by the lapels and put our hopes into action.

Tommy got it going and was our first chairman, while I was on the first committee we set up. When Ian St John took the chair he asked me if I'd be secretary. I agreed and I did that for eight years until I had the great honour of being made chairman.

We meet for golf days, dinners and other events, and make lots of money for charity. The corresponding organisation at Goodison, the Everton Former Players' Foundation, is a registered charity. It looks after the needs of the club's old players, ranging from supplying them with televisions to paying for medical operations – a worthy cause indeed.

Their organisation is chaired by my friend Laurence Lee, a distinguished Liverpool solicitor, who had a chat with me about our association when they were forming one at Everton.

Ours, though, is completely different because rather than existing to aid former players, we make donations to Merseyide charities, mainly those for children.

But in 2009, following the tragic and untimely death from lung cancer of my former wife Linda, we decided to give proceeds to the Roy Castle Lung Cancer Foundation.*

Liverpool FC gives our association home match tickets for former players and their guests in a set area of the Main Stand, and on match days some of the former players will work in the Anfield lounges doing pre-match talks and question-and-answer sessions.

We have more than 70 members, spanning all the post-war generations, including two wonderful veterans well into their 80s.

Laurie Hughes, the England centre-half who starred in the 1946/47 championship-winning season, and Charlie Ashcroft, the goalkeeper whose 89 appearances for Liverpool included a couple as Cyril Sidlow's deputy in the 1947 title team, attended our last Christmas party at the respective ages of 85 and 83! I was sad to hear about Charlie's death in March.

The camaraderie between us is superb. We have meetings about every two months in one of the hospitality boxes at Anfield and I'm delighted to say that Christian Purslow, not long after his appointment as the club's managing director, arranged a meeting with a representative group from the former players.

It was something we deeply appreciated and Christian is very keen for us to be involved right around the club. He realises that former players are part of the club's history and heritage.

However, relations have not always been sweetness and light. Rafael Benitez's predecessor Gerard Houllier took a distinct dislike to some of our members who work in the media.

He wasn't too happy with some of their public comments and he became paranoid about it, to such an extent that Ian St John was told he wasn't welcome at Anfield and couldn't work in the lounges.

It's a fact that there are more former Liverpool players than from any other club engaged in the media in some form at some level, ranging from the likes of Alan Hansen and Mark Lawrenson on national television to Tommy Smith having his say in his local newspaper column.

They are paid to give their opinions. If they held back when criticism is justified, just because they once played for the club, then they would be dishonest.

Monsieur Houllier, though, clearly felt it was an act of near treachery for the lads to say what they thought. I am happy to say that Ian St John and the other lads are all welcome again at Anfield and no such obstacles or feelings of resentment have come from Rafael Benitez.

We are very fortunate to have a wonderful "go between" in Brian Hall, himself a former player and team-mate of mine and also an employee of the club as their public relations executive.

I would like also to pay tribute to Brian's personal assistant Sue Griffiths who, apart from her own duties, works very hard on behalf of the former players, sending letters and emails, making telephone calls, and also organising our matchday tickets.

She's been fanastic for us and has ensured the admin side of our association functions efficiently. I don't know what we'd do without her.

For details of how to make donations to the Roy Castle Lung Cancer Foundation, contact their office on 0151 254 7200. Or write to them at: The Roy Castle Centre, 4-6 Enterprise Way, Wavertree Technical Park, Liverpool L13 1FB.

Sorry Rushie...

Returning to my all-time best Liverpool XI, I know the selection of my front three will cause arguments and controversy because I can find no place for Kevin Keegan, John Toshack, Ian St John, John Barnes, Peter Thompson, Robbie Fowler, Michael Owen or even – wait for it – Ian Rush!

Kenny Dalglish and Billy Liddell must be there, which leaves one other place up front. Billy could – and did – play anywhere, but I'd have him on the right of my front three. I first saw him when I was a kid in the 1950s. I'll never forget the gasps of anticipation from the crowd whenever he got the ball.

They used to shout: "Give it to Billy", because they knew that whenever he got the ball something was always likely to happen, such as a ferocious shot or header.

Even near the end of his career, when he'd lost some of his searing pace, he still had tremendous strength. And to the day he retired in 1961 he retained his wonderful Corinthian image.

Billy, recommended to Liverpool before the war by then Anfield captain Matt Busby, was a sportsman to his fingertips, a gentleman of the game. Indeed, as a magistrate and accountant he was a pillar of the community as well as being a god to the supporters who stood on the Kop.

Billy could – and did – play in every department of the Liverpool team except goal, but he starred for Scotland on the left wing and was also one of only two players to be selected for Great Britain on the only two occasions a united UK side has taken to the field.

In May 1947 he played in a 6-1 win against the Rest of Europe at Hampden Park, and in August 1955 in a 4-1 defeat by the Rest of Europe at Windsor Park, Belfast.

The only other player who appeared in both games was Stanley – later Sir Stanley – Matthews, the so-called "Wizard of the Dribble" himself. Not even the great Tom Finney – now Sir Tom – made the line-up. So that gives some indication of just how great Billy was.

In full majesty, flying down the flank, he was likened by one pundit to "an unstoppable red fire engine", and woe betide any defender who stepped in his path.

Yet despite his forceful, powerful 5ft 11in physique, he was never booked. And off the field he was so quietly spoken that you had to concentrate hard to hear what he said.

It was tremendously sad for Liverpool and English football that the final six seasons of Billy's Anfield career were spent outside the league's top flight, during the club's twilight years in the old-style Second Division following relegation after finishing bottom of Division One in 1953/54.

The gloom over the Kop when that happened was thickened by Everton's promotion back to the top flight as Liverpool made the drop.

It was hugely down to Billy, though, that things didn't get even worse with an unthinkable fall into the Third Division – a fear heightened by Liverpool's failure to win an away league game until February, a run that included a club record 9-1 December defeat at Birmingham.

But Billy's 30 league goals, after being switched to centre-forward in place of Louis Bimpson, stabilised things and Liverpool finished in 11th place... their lowest ever final league position. No wonder Liverpool was nicknamed "Liddellpool".

When Bill Shankly arrived as manager in December 1959 Billy's career was at its lowest ebb. He made only 12 first-team appearances for his former Scotland colleague, and within 18 months hung up his boots, being chaired off the pitch by teammates in his final outing for the reserves.

I had the privilege of playing in the reserves with Billy and then the honour of replacing him when I made my first-team debut against Bristol Rovers in April 1960. Later, our paths crossed again when I sat with him on the Spot The Ball panel, and when he stepped down I succeeded him as chairman.

What made Billy's achievements all the more astonishing was the fact that because his day job was in accountancy he was only a part-time professional at Anfield. It makes Roy of the Rovers believable!

Bob Paisley, who played left-half behind Billy in the Liverpool team, said that although he believed comparisons were odious he would make an exception for Billy Liddell. "He'd be priceless in any era of football," said Bob. I couldn't put it better than that.

Bob also said that during his half-century at Anfield he'd seen nobody better than Kenny Dalglish. Indeed, many long-time supporters hail King Kenny as the best player ever to pull on a Liverpool jersey.

When Kevin Keegan left for Hamburg in 1977, the prophets of doom were declaring him irreplaceable. But that was totally disproved by Kenny's arrival at Anfield, due in large part to Bob's friendship with the great Celtic manager Jock Stein who promised him that if Kenny left Parkhead it would be to Anfield.

Has there ever been a shrewder piece of business than that done by our chairman John Smith and chief executive Peter Robinson to sell Kevin for £500,000, sign Kenny to replace him and bank a £60,000 profit?

Kenny and the Kop were made for each other. A phenomenal player and a gifted manager, his period in charge came to an end when the terrible consequences of the Hillsborough disaster took a long-term toll on his health and forced him to quit in 1991.

His return to the club in 2009 as an Anfield ambassador and Academy consultant was warmly welcomed.

Kenny's potent attacking partnership with Ian Rush was one of the greatest – perhaps THE greatest – ever seen in English football, and Rushie, who was a terrific footballer as well as being a lethal finisher, is a strong contender for the last place in my team.

I have narrowed it down to picking Rushie or my former team-mate Roger Hunt, the World Cup winner bestowed with the title "Sir Roger" by the Kop. Oh, why can't I pick 12?! It's a cruel choice.

They were both phenomenal strikers, Rushie being the club's record scorer in an all competitions with 346 goals and Roger holding the league record with 245.

Simply because I played with Roger and know first hand of his great ability, he edges into my team ahead of Rushie. So the team, in 4-3-3 formation, reads:

Ray Clemence

Phil Neal   Alan Hansen   Tommy Smith (captain)   Gerry Byrne

Steven Gerrard   Graeme Souness   Ray Kennedy

Billy Liddell   Kenny Dalglish   Roger Hunt

My seven substitutes are: *Ian Rush, John Barnes, Kevin Keegan, Ian St John, Emlyn Hughes, Tommy Lawrence, Jamie Carragher*

Finally, my choice as my best ever Liverpool player. It comes down to three whose qualities I have already extolled... **Billy Liddell, Steven Gerrard** and **Kenny Dalglish.**

I could make a convincing case for each of them as my number one. But I'm going to opt for **Steven Gerrard** because he has such a massive influence on matches and those around him.

Shirt with a mystery tale

Little did I know when I headed home from London in the glorious aftermath of England's 1966 World Cup win that the shirt I had worn in the tournament would spark the biggest mystery of my football career.

But that's exactly what happened to the No 20 jersey I was allocated by England and which I wore with pride in our 2-0 win over France at Wembley in the group stage of the finals.

I have never been one to hoard memorabilia of my career, and over the years I've given away FA Cup final and European final shirts to friends who I knew would appreciate them and look after them.

And that's what I thought I had done with my World Cup jersey. But now I am baffled about exactly what happened to it.

Although England won the World Cup playing in red in the final against West Germany, we wore white jerseys against France.

To be honest I don't know what happened to my jersey. But, remarkably, some 35 years later I was at a dinner party given by my co-author John Keith and his wife Pat in Southport when two of the other guests, Duncan and Julie Swash, opened a bag and produced... my No 20 shirt!

They asked me to sign it, which I was delighted to do. I assumed Duncan and Julie had been given the jersey by Duncan's father Harold, a golf club manufacturer and a "putting doctor" who coached several top players including Nick Faldo.

Harold was a member at Hillside and had been heavily involved in getting the club to stage my testimonial golf day in 1978. I thought I had given him my jersey as a thank you.

But it transpires that the shirt had been in Duncan's family's possession since shortly after the 1966 World Cup when his grandfather, who had worked for the FA, was presented with my No 20 jersey. I had no idea. I knew nothing about that.

Another six years went by after that dinner party when suddenly my shirt popped up again... on national television!

When BBC TV's Antiques Roadshow visited Southport in February 2007, Julie took the signed shirt to show it to one of the programme's experts.

During the course of a six-minute feature on the jersey I was surprised to learn that it was valued at between £8,000 and £12,000.

But what happened to it after I took it off in the Wembley dressing room on the night of 20 July 1966 baffles me.

I understand the jersey is carefully wrapped in protective tissue paper at the Swash residence. And the mystery it has sparked is wrapped up with it.

Let's restore the glitter to the grand old FA Cup

One of the records of which I'm extremely proud – and which I discovered only recently – is that I have played more FA Cup games than any other player in history. What I'm not proud of is the way modern football regards the most romantic football competition in the world.

I learned that I'd made 88 appearances, comprising 79 for Liverpool, seven for Swansea and two for Crewe. And I'm delighted I was persuaded to go to Crewe because playing for them in the FA Cup kept me just one ahead of another former Liverpool player, John Barnes, in the all-time total.

When you consider that the FA Cup is the world's oldest knock-out competition, the first ball being kicked way back in November 1871, it's a distinction that gives me a great personal thrill.

But I'm not thrilled at all at the way many big clubs treat the competition today. It's an almost contemptuous attitude, many playing vastly weakened teams as if the FA Cup is an imposition on their season's programme which crystalises into a scramble for

either Champions League or Europa League places.

The FA Cup, I'm afraid, has become the victim of football's greed, of the pursuit of mega bucks which has made even finishing fourth a cause for a lap of honour. Fourth? Shankly and Paisley would turn in their graves if we'd celebrated that!

The FA Cup has always had a magic for me, from the time as a kid when I would get up early on cup final day and watch the build-up on television, to becoming a professional and playing in the competition.

I'll never forget the experience after training of sitting with my team-mates round a radio – or the wireless as it was known early in my career – and listening to the balls being shaken in a velvet bag at FA headquarters, waiting for the draw to be made. You were full of anticipation and expectation.

And when I got to play for Liverpool in the 1965 final against Leeds, and helped us win the cup for the first time, it was on a par with the 1977 European Cup final win as the greatest day of my football life.

Playing at Wembley has also been devalued. It used to be reserved for internationals and cup finals. To reach an FA Cup final was one of the finest achievements for a player and one that eluded so many greats of the game, George Best and Gordon Banks to name but two.

Now, with play-offs and semi-finals being staged there, it is no longer special. Like the taxi owner who has to keep the wheels of his cab turning to earn money, so Wembley is thrown open to get a return on the investment in the new stadium.

As for the FA Cup, it's part of our national heritage and it's a scandal the way it has fallen down the pecking order. As I said earlier, it's down to one word – money.

So let's put the FA Cup back on its rightful pedestal by awarding the FA Cup winners a place in the Champions League qualifiers instead of the fourth-placed team in the league.

I don't think you'd see weakened teams paraded then!

Bobby wanted us all to share in glory of 1966

Iconic is a word that has almost lost its meaning, given its over-use and misuse today. Yet, if one image can be said to be an icon of English football it is surely that of England captain Bobby Moore, chaired by his jubilant red-shirted team-mates, thrusting the freshly won World Cup into the Wembley air on that July day in 1966.

With his blond locks and athletic physique, Bobby was an Adonis who could have come straight from central casting to fill the captain's role. But there was nothing theatrical about Bobby.

What you saw was what you got – a superb player and an equally brilliant captain. Given recent controversy over what is required of an England captain, the qualities Bobby brought to the job stand out as gold-plated – the level to which all others must aspire.

I had already played against Bobby in Liverpool v West Ham games before I really got to appreciate his abilities of skill and leadership when we were in the 1966 World Cup squad. I've talked elsewhere about how he made sure that the entire 22-man squad received an equal £1,000 share of the World Cup prize money.

Not for him selfish thoughts about what he could get. He was concerned that every player, whether they'd appeared in the tournament or not, would be treated equally.

That was his style of captaincy. And on and off the field he was the definition of cool and nothing would faze him.

Everything had to be right, everything in its place – so much so that Alan Ball revealed that Bobby would iron his paper money then fold the notes and keep them in a gold clip.

Bobby quite rightly won the Player of the Tournament award in the 1966 World Cup, and before the 1970 World Cup, when the Colombian authorities trumped up ridiculous theft allegations against him over an emerald bracelet, he came through it with his usual unruffled style.

He then proceeded to give a master class in the art of defensive play when the tournament began, typified by that amazing clean-as-a-whistle tackle on Pele, who hailed him as "the best defender in the world".

Bobby wasn't the quickest of players but the fact that he always seemed to have space around him revealed his razor-sharp football brain.

Whenever we would meet, in the days long after we'd both hung up our boots, Bobby would always be genuinely interested in how I was and what I was doing. He was a special human being.

Like Alan Ball and Brian Labone, he left us far too early, in Bobby's case at the age of only 51, when he succumbed to cancer in 1993.

He left behind a peerless legacy, a role model of captaincy that will echo down the generations.

Why I have a grouse with Partridge

In almost 1,000 games in senior football there is just one booking against my name. It's a disciplinary record I'm proud of and one which would be impossible in today's game.

Yet the one caution I did receive has always rankled with me. It happened in Liverpool's League Cup final replay against Nottingham Forest at Old Trafford in March 1978.

Shortly before the interval, a ball bounced between Peter Withe and me. Peter was a big lad, well over six feet tall. I accidentally – and I stress accidentally – caught him in the chest and he went down.

Referee Pat Partridge came over and booked me, despite my honest explanation that it was an accident and appeals from my fellow Scouser Peter not to caution me.

Even Liverpool as a club tried to have the booking expunged but Mr Partridge, from Cockfield, County Durham, stood by his decision. Perhaps he wanted my name to help make a name for himself.

During the subsequent 32 years I've been in his company only once, at a golf club function, and unfortunately the circumstances weren't right for me to raise the matter with him.

He hardly covered himself in glory on that midweek night in Manchester. Early in the second half he blew for a foul by Phil Thompson on John O'Hare, which was clearly a yard outside the box.

But to our utter amazement he gave Forest a penalty. He wouldn't listen to our protests and John Robertson sent his spot-kick past Ray Clemence – agonisingly brushing Clem's fingertips on its way in – for the only goal of the tie, the Wembley game the previous Saturday having finished goalless.

So Brian Clough's Forest lifted the trophy through that clearly wrong decision and whenever I recall my only booking my sense of injustice is not just personal. It's for the whole team.

To let you into a secret, almost three years before that Forest game I had my name taken in a pre-season friendly against Borussia Dortmund in Germany. I was cautioned by referee Helmut Bartnik, although I cannot recall why.

But the booking never went beyond the referee's notebook. It was not reported officially and didn't stand against what was then my unblemished discliplinary record.

To be honest, my booking by Pat Partridge did have a positive spin-off because it proved a talking point and drew attention to the fact that over the course of my long career it was my only caution. It was the exception that proved the rule.

I'm sure that if I played now I'd collect far more than a single booking and I think the days are long gone when anyone could repeat the feats of Merseyside greats Dixie Dean (497 career games) and Billy Liddell (522 career games), neither of whom collected a single caution.

The disciplinary clampdown, which renders you liable to be booked for silly things let alone tackling from behind, makes it almost inevitable that most players – even the least malicious – pick up yellow cards and that a significant number see red.

Thanks for the headache, Fernando!

Now you may be wondering, having seen my dream Liverpool team, why there is no place for Fernando Torres. I have to admit that it's not only on the field that he causes problems... he gave me a massive headache, too.

Let me make it clear that there is no question whatsoever that Fernando deserves his inclusion. He's a sensational striker. My problem was that I didn't know who to leave out to put him in. And that's the honest, awkward truth.

Indeed, I cannot recall any Liverpool striker – and none at any other club for that matter – with the same pace over long distances that the Spaniard possesses.

Roger Hunt, Ian Rush, Kenny Dalglish, Robbie Fowler, Michael Owen were superb forwards but you cannot compare them to Torres. He's a one-off. He's got exceptional skill and I have never seen a Liverpool player with such speed.

It is quite remarkable how he can take the ball off opponents and just leave them standing, trailing in his wake. He scores goals with feet and head from any angle.

Two of his many great goals stand out for me. One was his fantastic strike at home against Blackburn in April 2009 when he chested down a Jamie Carragher cross on the right of the box and hit a superb right-footed, angled, over-the-shoulder shot that flew past Paul Robinson. Eat your heart out Marco Van Basten!

The other was against Manchester United at Anfield in October 2009 when, despite being less than fully match fit, he swept onto Yossi Benayoun's pass, fended off Rio Ferdinand's attempt to push him off the ball and fired past a stunned Edwin Van Der Saar into the Kop net.

To leave the England centre-back a straggler, as Torres did, exemplified both his strength and his pace. He also takes a huge amount of physical stick from defenders.

And while some people criticise him for complaining to referees too often, I don't blame him. I don't think they realise just how much stick he takes from opponents.

I had virtually picked my all-time Liverpool team, from players who had been at the club many years. Then along came this lad who opened up a new dimension in attacking play.

He's one of the best in the world and he's sorely missed by Liverpool whenever he's out injured. There's no doubt that if he stays at Anfield he can become a legend among legends, a Kop hero to rival any of the past.

I'm sure nobody would fancy coming up against this team

I've picked my best Liverpool team and that was hard enough, but I discovered another tough challenge I was given when I came across an old newspaper cutting from the Liverpool Echo recently. The year was 1977 and I was asked to pick an all-star team from all the footballers I had played with – excluding Liverpool players. After much thought, this was the team I produced, in 4-2-4 formation.

GOALKEEPER: GORDON BANKS

The best goalkeeper I've ever seen. I played in the England team with him in 1966. To my mind he is probably the best goalkeeper there has ever been. It was a tragedy when he had to give up the game because of his accident. I remember his last match well – it was at Anfield and I scored what turned out to be the last goal he conceded.

RIGHT-BACK: ALEX PARKER

I watched him play many times for Everton. He was very quick, and his distribution was very impressive. He could pinpoint his passes, and that made him an exceptional defender.

CENTRE-BACK: COLIN TODD

His distribution is great, although he hasn't done as well for England as he has for his club. The Colin Todd of three or four years ago was a tremendous player – and in my opinion he is still a great player.

CENTRE-BACK: BOBBY MOORE

One of the best back-four players I have ever seen; in fact, one of the greatest players of all. He was a master of his own particular game, and had the same majesty on the ball as Beckenbauer.

LEFT-BACK: RAY WILSON

Probably the quickest left-back I have played against. When I was very young I played against him a couple of times when he was with Huddersfield, and then again when he joined Everton. In those days I was a winger; that's why I am so sure about him. He wasn't very tall, but that didn't handicap him at all.

MIDFIELD: JOHNNY GILES

I don't think I have seen a better passer of the ball than Giles. The space he creates for himself is unbelievable. He had a great knowledge of the game, which he used to the full.

MIDFIELD: BILLY BREMNER

I would pick him for his sheer enthusiasm for the game, and the way he made people around him tick. On top of that he was a great player himself. To some extent, I think his footballing ability was underestimated. People were so aware of his talent as a motivator that they tended to overlook that aspect of his game.

ATTACK: GEORGE BEST

The best player I have ever played against. No hesitation about that. I like everything about him – he could score goals, create them, work hard. Magic. There was one season when he carried United, when they were having to struggle he kept them up near the top of the table. In a team game it's an impossibility, but he did it.

ATTACK: BOBBY CHARLTON

The most graceful player I have seen. With the ball at his feet he had so much balance. He was one of the best passers of the ball, particularly over long distances, and scored some fantastic goals from 30 to 35 yards.

ATTACK: DENIS LAW

One of the best in the 18-yard box. His ability to snap up half-chances from impossible angles and positions made him outstanding, and he was as good with his head as his feet. Players like that don't come along these days.

ATTACK: JIMMY GREAVES

The most prolific goalscorer I have played against. He scored goals with so much ease it was untrue, and he did it week in, week out. It didn't matter which club he was with, he still scored a lot of goals. Gordon Milne tells a story of how he played for Preston against Chelsea one day. He was told to mark Greaves, and he followed him everywhere. But at the end of the match, Greaves had scored five goals. That's the type of player he was.

The day Jimmy basked in my derby glory

I played against Everton 31 times and every single game had those special derby ingredients... frenzy, passion and pride.

Sometimes, in the more physical encounters, the ball was almost incidental. On other occasions it was like a hot potato that players couldn't get rid of quick enough.

My third senior encounter with Everton was very special for me because I scored both goals in our 2-1 win at Anfield on 28 September 1963.

They were the only derby goals I ever scored... but Jimmy Melia refused to let me take all the plaudits!

The Liverpool team was: Tommy Lawrence, Gerry Byrne, Phil Ferns, Gordon Milne, Ron Yeats, Willie Stevenson, myself, Roger Hunt, Ian St John, Jimmy Melia and Peter Thompson.

Everton lined up with Gordon West in goal, Alex Parker, Sandy Brown, Tony Kay, Brian Labone, Brian Harris, Alex Scott, Dennis Stevens, Derek Temple, Roy Vernon and Johnny Morrissey.

My goals straddled the half-time interval, my first coming in the

43rd minute. Jimmy Melia gave me a short pass of no more than four yards.

I came in on it and whacked it from 25 yards and it flew into the top corner of Westy's net. Although I say it myself, it was a cracker!

The second one came in strange fashion three minutes into the second half. Jimmy was almost on top of me when he planted the ball at my feet.

This time I mishit my shot and the ball just bobbled towards the goal-line. Westy, instead of picking it up, decided he'd kick it clear. But he failed to connect with the ball and it just trickled into the net.

It didn't matter to me how it had gone in. I was delighted to have scored twice in a five-minute spell against our arch-rivals.

But when I got back to the dressing room, Jimmy came over and said: "Hey, Cal. I don't half lay the goals on for you, don't I!"

I was, as they say, gobsmacked. But I couldn't really say anything. I was just a young lad then and Jimmy was an established pro, a fine player who was capped by England, later to win new fame as the white-shoed Brighton manager who led them to the 1983 FA Cup final against Manchester United and later moved into American soccer.

But in the ensuing years we've had a laugh about that derby day when I scored twice... and Jimmy basked in reflected glory!

I haven't hung up my boots – I've thrown them away

After my agreed short period playing for Cork and the unfortunate outcome of the interest from Norway, it was back to the pub business with Geoff Strong. I'd finally retired from football – or so I thought.

I was labouring at the Golden Lion to help get the place ready for its refurbished re-opening when I got a call from my long-time pal and former team-mate Alan A'Court, who was assistant at Crewe to manager Arfon Griffiths. Arfon's a great guy and still a good friend of mine today.

"How about coming to Crewe for a month, Cally?" Alan asked me. "We need a wise, old head in midfield."

"Alan, I'm sorry," I replied. "I've not only hung up my boots – I've thrown them away!"

But in very short order, Alan arrived at the pub to talk to me in person and try to make me change my mind. And because of what I thought of Alan, and being appreciative of how he'd taken me under his wing when I was a young player, that's exactly what I did.

I would drive through to train twice a week and ended up playing for Crewe from October 1981 to the following March, making 15 appearances in Division Four.

My last ever professional outing, a month before my 40th birthday, was at Halifax Town when we lost 2-1, Mark Palios scoring our goal.

It ended my career and an enjoyable five-month spell at Crewe which meant that I had played in all four divisions of the Football League.

The six months that seemed like rainbow's end

Patience is a virtue... it all comes to he who waits... the sayings and platitudes are many. Yet in my case, seven months of my life, more than 14 years after my Liverpool debut, were just unbelievable.

Between May 1974 and the end of that year I collected five individual awards and then found myself with an MBE in the New Year Honours List.

I couldn't quite take in this cascade of honours. I was quite happy being a team player, helping the side win and, hopefully, collecting a winner's medal or two.

But that all changed in 1974, beginning with a dinner at Liverpool's Adelphi Hotel when I was presented with the Merseyside Sportsman of the Year Award organised by the Liverpool Echo.

That was followed by Granada TV's Kick Off award, which was decided through a ballot of my fellow north-west professionals, while readers of the Daily Express voted me as their Player of the Year, as did readers of The Sun.

Then came news that stunned me. The Football Writers' Association announced that they had voted me as Footballer of the Year, the most prestigious individual trophy in the English game, dating back to 1948 when Stanley Matthews was the first recipient of the award.

I had always associated it, rightly or wrongly, with a well-known international player, a household name. Although I'd had a good season in 1973/74, I didn't do anything more individually than I'd done in other seasons.

Yet perhaps I won the award – the first time a Liverpool player had done so – because the game had been going through a bad period with misbehaviour on the terraces and on the field.

People were pointing out that I'd been playing for 14 years without having my name taken. The fact that I had a clean record was something out of the ordinary and it was highlighted at a time when football was cloaked in negative publicity.

But winning the award changed my outlook and from then on I considered the Footballer of the Year as recognition of the all-round qualities of a player, not just the amount of stardust he generates. Or, I hope that's what the writers consider when they vote.

I learned I'd won it a week before our FA Cup final against Newcastle. I was in London with the team for our league game at West Ham, and on the Friday evening I went with some of the lads to see a film in the West End.

I was just going to bed when Bill Shankly told me that ITV's World of Sport wanted to do an interview with me next morning. The boss, who'd obviously given the go-ahead for me to do it, said: "You won't be too long. They're calling for you at 11 o'clock and you'll be back here before 12." So, next day I was collected and taken to the studio.

I waited for about 15 minutes, drinking a cup of coffee, then went in to meet Brian Moore who said he'd like a chat about the cup final a week later.

We were about to start the interview when, from behind some curtains, stepped Mike Langley of the Sunday People, the chairman of the FWA, holding the Footballer of the Year trophy!

I was speechless. I could hardly take in what was going on. I'd been set up in best This Is Your Life tradition. When I got myself together as best I could, Mike explained that the award would be officially presented the following Thursday at the FWA's annual dinner in London.

So, with my head still spinning, I was taken back to the team's hotel to leave for Upton Park. None of the lads knew what had happened and Emlyn Hughes came over to me and said he'd heard that Billy Bremner had won the award.

"Oh, no he hasn't," I told Emlyn. "I've just been to collect it now!" Billy came second to me, with Emlyn in third place, and Kevin Keegan also figured in the voting.

The presentation dinner was less than 48 hours before our FA Cup final against Newcastle at Wembley. Earlier in the day I travelled south with the team to our pre-Wembley base at St Albans before Shanks and I took a taxi to the dinner where I would formally receive the famous statuette.

On the way I kept glancing at the notes I'd prepared for my acceptance speech, for which I'd had great help from Tom Saunders, the club's youth development officer who I'd known since my schoolboy days.

The prospect of speaking to hundreds in that room was nerve-wracking and daunting. But just before we walked into the dining hall Shanks said the magic words: "Don't worry son... you get out of this game only what you put into it."

That calmed me instantly. I sat on the top table betweeen football administrators Sir Stanley Rous and Len Shipman, and my speech went down well. It was a night that will live with me forever.

So will my trip to Buckingham Palace to receive my MBE. Liverpool FC booked my wife Lin, our first daughter Samantha and myself into a hotel near the palace and we travelled down the day before the investiture.

After we'd checked in, my pal Jimmy Tarbuck sent a car with his driver to pick us up and take us to a dinner party at his house in Surrey to celebrate my MBE.

Cilla Black and Bernie Winters – half of the comedy duo Mike and Bernie – were among the guests and we had a great time.

Next day, at the appointed time, Lin, Samantha and I were off to the palace to see the Queen! You're told what form the ceremony takes and to speak when you're spoken to.

Her Majesty bestows the honours to the recipients in alphabetical order. While Lin and Samantha sat in the audience I waited for my turn to be called.

It's exciting and nerve-wracking at the same time. Then came the moment when I walked forward, briefly bowed my head as instructed, and received my award.

The Queen said something to me but I have no recollection of what she said. It was lost in that heady moment.

Footsteps in the fog and the Porsche generation

The recruitment and treatment of young players has changed dramatically since I used to catch the bus from our Toxteth tenement to train as an amateur two nights a week at Melwood, after I'd got my first job as a trainee French polisher.

In those days of the 1950s, any lad who came from outside Merseyside was looked on almost as a foreigner and the situation was similar at most English clubs. Now the kids come from the other side of the world and all points in between.

And instead of travelling by bus, the mode of transport for aspiring youngsters as they sweep in and out of the state-of-the-art Premier League club academies is by luxury Mercedes, BMW or Porsche.

Let me make clear that I feel no envy for them. My own formative years in football paved the way to a career that I couldn't even have dreamed of. But I do have two massive concerns about where modern football is going in the area of youth development.

First, how many boys come through to make it at Premier League level? And, second, the small number of British – let alone English – graduates to the top level is dwindling to the extent that it must have a massively negative impact on the ambitions of our own youngsters who harbour the dreams I once had.

In Liverpool's case the question has to be asked: where are the successors to Robbie Fowler, Michael Owen, Steven Gerrard and Jamie Carragher, all of whom emerged before the advent of the academy system?

I'll never forget training in freezing fog at Melwood one evening in late February 1958, just three weeks after the loss of so many of Manchester United's Busby Babes in the Munich air disaster.

After the training session I left Melwood and walked to the bus stop to get the bus home. As I was standing there, perishing in the gloom, a bloke walking past said to me: "No use waiting there, mate. All the buses are off because of the fog."

It meant only one thing... I had to walk the eight miles home, knowing my mum and dad would be wondering where I was. I had no way of telling them. It was decades before mobile phones and it was no use stopping at a call box because we didn't have a phone at home.

That wintry scenario was by no means an isolated experience for aspiring boys like me who had ambitions of making it in professional football. It is on a different planet from the money and luxury now lavished on youngsters expensively groomed for a career at the top but who, too often, never make their target level.

With every crushed dream for an English youngster, the future of the international side and the country's prestige becomes even more problematical as it battles to keep its head above the growing tide of foreign players.

And it seems absurd that Premier League academy rules dictate that a club cannot sign a British youngster who lives outside a 90-mile radius of the club when they bring them in for substantial fees from anywhere from Rio to Timbuktu. With it have come accusations and allegations that some clubs have been guilty of illegal inducements to young foreign players.

I am not someone who looks back with rose-tinted glasses. But I do have a deep concern about the state of today's youth coaching and development, and England's future as a world football power.

To be frank, kids today are mollycoddled, isolated and cocooned from the real game.

When you examine the millions of pounds spent and numbers of staff employed at the Premier League academies, you must question the value of the investment – not only in time and money, but also the effect it has on the boys.

In no way am I saying that everything in my young days was better. Far from it. We had to put up with all sorts of things that I'm glad today's kids don't have to contend with.

Yet, overall, our experiences were character-forming as well as educational in a football sense.

However dedicated the youth coaches are – and I've nothing but admiration for most of those I've encountered – it is a hell of a difficult job to prepare youngsters for the hard world of professional football within the comparatively cloistered existence of the academies.

How different it was when I was learning the game. And at the risk of being accused of allowing distance to lend enchantment, I'm sure my formative experience was far more beneficial than the cosy way today's youngsters are treated.

Scots and Scousers: Where are the next Billy Liddell or Robbie Fowler coming from?

I fear that these prize breeds face Kop extinction

A trawl through Liverpool FC history will show that two groups of players have filled major roles in the club's remarkable success, which embraces 18 league titles (although none since 1990 and none at all in the Premier League era), five European Cup triumphs, three UEFA Cup wins and seven each in the FA Cup and League Cup.

I'm talking about Scots and Scousers. The first team Liverpool paraded in the late 19th century included 10 Scottish players, and down the generations the tartan influence has been prominent in Liverpool teams.

Anfield has been blessed with great Scots, including Matt McQueen in the 1890s; Alex Raisbeck in the early 1900s; Don McKinlay, who had a 19-year career through to the late 1920s; Tom Bradshaw, Jim McDougall and Matt Busby in the 1930s; Billy Liddell in the 1940s and '50s; Ian St John, Ron Yeats and

Willie Stevenson in the 1960s; and Kenny Dalglish, Graeme Souness and Alan Hansen in the 1970s and '80s.

The late Liverpool chairman Sir John Smith used to say: "Liverpool win nothing without Scottish players." However, thanks to the trophies gathered by Rafael Benitez's Scots-free teams, Smith's assertion has been shown not to be strictly correct – the final Scottish flag to fly in the Liverpool side was lowered when Gary McAllister departed.

Now, the supply line of top Scottish talent into English football has become a trickle, and until the football authorities north of the border find a method of turning on the tap again, the current situation is unlikely to change.

But we face a similar headache on our own doorstep. When Steven Gerrard and Jamie Carragher end their careers, where are the local boys to follow in their illustrious footsteps and in the tradition set by the likes of Gerry Byrne, Chris Lawler, Tommy Smith, Sammy Lee, Robbie Fowler and all the other Mersey-born players who have brought honour to Anfield?

Stevie and Jamie – who were products of the old pre-Academy youth development system – have been hailed by Benitez as "the heart of the team", but I fear that Scouse heart will stop beating when those two step down from the action.

With the number of foreigners in our game it's difficult enough for any Brits to break through, let alone specifically Scousers, and without some local blood in the side Liverpool just wouldn't be the same.

Let us hope some other lads from Huyton or Bootle or somewhere else on Merseyside will have the talent to illuminate the Anfield stage and keep alive a distinguished line.

Replacing Stevie toughest job of the lot

At some stage in the future – and I sincerely hope a long way into the distance – a Liverpool manager, whoever he may be, is going to have to face one of the toughest moments of truth to befall any incumbent of that office... the end of Steven Gerrard's Anfield career.

I have outlined in this book, in selecting the Liverpool team of my lifetime, that Stevie is the best of any of the club's players I have lined up with or watched, which, when you consider the likes of Liddell, Dalglish, Keegan, Souness and other greats who have donned the Anfield red with distinction down the decades, is the finest tribute I can pay him.

It is a truth honed by time that nobody is indispensable and it applies to football as it does to any other walk of life. The prophets of doom were in full flow when Bill Shankly sensationally quit in the summer of 1974, predicting he was an impossible act to follow and that Liverpool's demise was imminent.

Nine years and 19 trophies later, Bob Paisley had rammed those forecasts down their throats and out the other end! Likewise, when

Kevin Keegan upped sticks and headed for his "new challenge" in Hamburg, the pundits declared that the Liverpool machine had lost an irreplaceable cog... then along came Kenny Dalglish.

Ray Clemence's departure, they predicted, would leave a big hole in Liverpool's defensive armour until Bruce Grobbelaar revealed a new style of goalkeeping that was showered with silverware. Ian Rush's exit for pastures new at Juventus led to Liverpool parading an attacking force of John Barnes, Peter Beardsley and John Aldridge, which gave us football of such breathtaking quality that many still rate it the finest that any Liverpool side has ever produced.

So Liverpool have traditionally shown extraordinary powers of replacement and regeneration. But those powers are going to be tested like never before when Steven Gerrard either leaves or hangs up his boots, simply because he is the complete footballer.

Wherever he's played, whether it be central midfield, out on the flank or as a support striker, he's been exceptional. Billy Liddell was once persuaded by Ronnie Moran not to take over as emergency goalkeeper in a game on the basis that he was far too valuable as an outfield player.

The same applies to Stevie... but he has so much natural talent that if he ever did go between the posts I would expect him to be at least proficient and probably impressive.

He has, as they say, got the lot. He's a goalscorer, he's a defender, he can head the ball, he's got pace, he can go past people, he's hard and he makes things happen. When you examine his abilities, you have to say there's nothing that guy can't do.

With no disrespect to a midfield great like Graeme Souness, he couldn't do some of the things that Stevie does. Graeme was a fantastic player, but he didn't score the goals Stevie does and he

didn't have his pace.

Stevie's up there with the world's best and he would have walked into any of the great Liverpool teams whether it be the '60s, '70s or '80s. And Shankly and Paisley would have drooled over having a player like him. But one day their latest successor is going to have to face life without Stevie in the team. I don't envy him!

RECEPTION

Outside
Melwood,
Liverpool's
training
ground

What the legends said about a legend called Cally

I WAS GLAD TO GET PAST HIM – GEORGE BEST

I played against Cally many times and watched him on television before we found ourselves team-mates and room-mates at Fort Lauderdale in the United States.

What struck me about him was the fact that he ran round like a kid, even though he'd been playing for years and years. He was able to do that because of his absolute, 100% dedication to football.

He never stopped running and chasing, and in United v Liverpool games he was someone I was always glad to get past. If I did that, I'd no worries.

I'd have liked to have been in Ian's situation of not having all the pressures outside the game, because the lack of them helps a player enormously.

I never believed in comparing one player with another. It's enough to say that Ian Callaghan was a great one.

HE LISTENED TO THE GOSPEL – BILL SHANKLY

A manager's dream... that's Ian Callaghan. He's a model man and model player. Ian's switch to midfield came late in his career and robbed him of many international appearances.

If it had happened several years earlier he'd have won 20 or 30 caps. I used to have to tell him to simmer down in training because he drove himself.

"You go through the motions, son," I'd say to him on the training ground. But to the others who were taking part in the same function, I'd say: "You'd better get it right or we're going to be here all day."

In my playing days, when we played for a pittance, I started looking forward to the next game the moment the final whistle blew. Ian Callaghan's attitude is the same.

How was he capable of what he achieved over such a long period? Because he listened to the gospel... the gospel of dedication and enthusiasm. He's a model man and model player, and will go down as one of the game's greats.

THE ONLY PERSON IN THE GAME WITHOUT A SINGLE ENEMY – KEVIN KEEGAN

When I joined Liverpool from Scunthorpe in 1971 I was immediately struck by how welcoming and friendly Ian Callaghan was towards me. I thought: "Give it time and I'll get to know him as he really is."

The fact is that the man I met as a newcomer IS the real Ian Callaghan. He must be the only person in the game without a single enemy. But he's much, much more than a very nice bloke.

He was a superbly consistent player. Sure, he'd have a bad game occasionally... like once every other season!

Considering that he played so well for Liverpool for so long and with such incredible consistency, I was staggered that it wasn't until late in his career that he began to receive the acclaim he deserved.

His enthusiasm for the game and his hard work were fantastic. He played football year after year with the same attitude as a raw, starry-eyed youngster.

A TRUE ROLE MODEL – BOB PAISLEY

If every player in the game was like Ian Callaghan there would be no managers left, simply because they wouldn't be needed.

To call him a great professional doesn't do him justice. In addition to his outstanding playing qualities, he never lost his temper, never got ruffled, never shouted the odds and never got carried away with anything.

And if you add up all that you are left with a true role model, an example of what all youngsters should aspire to.

I knew Ian from the time he joined Liverpool as an amateur in the 1950s, when he trained twice a week at Melwood, and his character and personality never changed.

He was the same then as he was on that wonderful night in Rome more than 20 years later when he was in the team that won the club's first European Cup. As a man and a player they come no greater than Ian Callaghan.

HE DIDN'T PACK UP, HE JUST CHANGED – IAN ST JOHN

When I joined Liverpool, Ian was only a teenager and he was a straightforward winger. He'd come back for the ball, take it along the line and get it over. That was his job... uncomplicated.

Directness and simplicity seemed to be his strength. I could never have imagined then that he would develop into the great midfield player he became.

Near the end of my time at Liverpool, Ian was beginning to tuck in as a kind of deep-lying winger before he progressed to the centre of midfield.

Suddenly, this boy who had never shown himself as a great tackler was running the show. And he made the switch at a stage in his career when many players would be thinking about packing up.

Now he's made another switch – to join our cast of The Bill Shankly Story stage show. And guess what? He's impressive in that, too!

A PLAYER'S PLAYER – HOWARD KENDALL

I always felt that Cally and Peter Thompson, as the wingers, were the vital people in the Liverpool team. I never imagined that he would drop back and become a midfielder.

But he did it so well that it looked as if he was tailor-made for the job. Cally had great involvement in the game... I don't know whether he revolved around the others or they revolved around him. The work he got through was terrific, not only on the ball – the situation in which most people seem to judge players – but also off it.

His knowledge of the game was fantastic. If Tommy Smith went on a run, Cally would fill in for him. If Emlyn Hughes or other defenders moved up you had to ask why they were never caught out. The answer is that Cally was there.

You had to play with or against him to appreciate how good a player he was. How would you describe him? Well, let's say he was an asset to the team, a player's player. There's no praise higher than that.

IT BAFFLED ME WHY HE WAS IGNORED BY ENGLAND – TOMMY SMITH

If a mother wanted her son to be a footballer, she'd want him to be like Cally. Sometimes you reflect on his life and career and think he's too good to be true – yet he is true.

I roomed with him for Liverpool and I know what a generous and modest man he is. As a player I was baffled why he was ignored by England from 1966 to 1977. Why he didn't receive more international recognition I'll never know.

He never sang his own praises yet he is to Liverpool what Bobby Charlton is to Manchester United and Tom Finney to Preston.

Ian was virtually beyond improvement as a player. He may not have been a great header of the ball, but then heading was not something he was called on to do very often.

His desire for hard work, this wanting to do everything himself, put him in a class of his own. And I'm proud to say I helped because every time we ran onto the pitch for a match I'd be right behind him giving his shoulders a rub!

SUPERB PROFESSIONAL – HARRY CATTERICK

When I was Everton manager and we played Liverpool, we tried to find ways of marking Ian. But it was very difficult to do because he was so quick and mobile. It was no easy task to pick him up. So many tributes have been paid to him that it's hard to add to them. I never saw him commit a deliberate foul nor remember him ever complaining on his own behalf.

He just went out on the field and got on with his game as the superb professional he was. It's a great pity that he won only two caps as a winger back in 1966 and had to wait 11 years to win another two as a midfielder. He deserved more.

I can't think of a better example of a man who gave everything he had in terms of effort, skill, loyalty and sportsmanship. If football had a few hundred players like Ian Callaghan the game would be in a wonderful state.

NOT FOR HIM A LIFE OF BOOZE AND FAGS
– BRIAN CLOUGH

Most people I have come across in football have given Ian Callaghan the "model professional" label. But that's an insult to him. It's been used TOO often to describe TOO many people for it to apply in Ian's case.

He's arguably the most genuine player the game has produced. So he deserves a special identity.

I didn't have much contact with Ian over the years... and that's a pity. I enjoy being associated with honest, reliable people, and they don't come any more faithful than him.

A player has to be really outstanding to be recalled by his country at the age of 35, but it was no surprise to me that it happened to Ian. No matter how much talent you have, you can never hope to be at the top as a footballer when you reach your mid-30s unless you set yourself certain standards.

Ian Callaghan not only set himself standards – he invented them. Not for him a life of booze and fags or any of the other vices that have ruined many a career. He got the rewards for looking after himself, working conscientiously and behaving in a proper manner.

Over the years there have been thousands of professionals who have abused themselves. They could have benefited from a fraction of the qualities Ian had to offer.

HIS LOVE OF FOOTBALL KEPT HIM GOING
– SIR BOBBY CHARLTON

I have a healthy respect for all good professionals and I don't think there is anyone in the game who could possibly have faulted Ian Callaghan as a player.

He had skill, positional sense, effort and showed great loyalty to Liverpool. He had a whole-hearted enthusiasm for the game and many players would be delighted to have his legs.

It was a matter of some amazement to many people that he kept going as he did right through his career. It's the love of football that was the main reason he carried on playing for so long.

His switch to midfield was a big success but, then, he was one of those players you could play anywhere. Put him at full back and he'd have done a good job. He was such a shrewd tactician.

Because of the Kop and Liverpool's effort as a team, people tended to overlook individual skills. Ian was a jack-of-all-trades... and a master of them all.

He will be remembered not just as a great club man but as a truly great player, and I was delighted that he won an England recall at the age of 35 and after 11 years out of international football.

Cally's amazing statistics

With LIVERPOOL

	Appearances	Goals
Football League:	640 (inc 4 sub)	50
FA Cup:	79 (inc 2 sub)	2
League Cup:	42	7
Europe:	89 (inc 1 sub)	10
Charity Shield:	7	0
TOTAL:	*857*	*69*

With SWANSEA

Football League	76	1
FA Cup:	7	0
League Cup:	4	0

With CREWE

Football League:	15	0
FA Cup:	2	0
League Cup:	0	0
OVERALL TOTAL:	*961*	*70*

Top 10 Liverpool appearances
(all competitions, with goals in brackets)

Ian Callaghan:	857 (69)
Emlyn Hughes:	665 (49)
Ray Clemence:	665 (0)
Ian Rush:	660 (346)
Phil Neal:	650 (59)
Tommy Smith:	639 (48)
Bruce Grobbelaar:	628 (0)
Alan Hansen:	620 (14)
Jamie Carragher:	613 (5)*
Chris Lawler:	549 (61)

(* still playing, figures as at 26 Feb 2010)

* Ian Callaghan is the most decorated member of England's 1966 World Cup-winning squad (see list below). Sir Bobby Charlton is next with 3 league title medals, 1 FA Cup, 2 FA Cup runners-up medals, 1 European Cup, English and European Footballer of the Year awards, and 2 Charity Shields.

* Callaghan won 4 England caps, 4 Under-23 caps and made 2 appearances for the Football League representative side. He was a member of England's 22-man World Cup-winning squad in 1966, appearing in the finals in the group game against France.

* His 857 appearances for Liverpool is a club record, and his 88 career FA Cup appearances is the most by any player in the competition's history.

He is the only Liverpool player to appear for Liverpool in the former Second Division and in a European Cup final.

His 857 appearances for Liverpool is the second highest for one club in senior competitions, surpassed only by John Trollope's 889 for Swindon Town between 1960 and 1980. At the time of publication, Manchester United's Ryan Giggs was closing in, having surpassed 800 appearances.

Liverpool never lost a league game in which Callaghan scored.

He scored one hat-trick: in the League Cup fourth-round replay against Hull City at Anfield on 4 December 1973.

He was the first Liverpool substitute to score in a European game, hitting the last of his side's four goals at Dundalk in the Fairs Cup first round second leg, 30 September 1969.

Callaghan captained Liverpool once, against Norwich City in the league game at Anfield, 2 February 1974, in recognition of his being voted Merseyside Sportsman of the Year.

Callaghan scored in six major competitions for Liverpool: league, FA Cup, League Cup, European Cup, Fairs Cup and Cup Winners' Cup. He also scored from the spot in the Charity Shield penalty shoot-out against Leeds at Wembley in 1974, which is not included in official goalscoring figures.

He wore six different numbered shirts for Liverpool: 7, 9, 10, 11, 12 and 14. He wore the 14 jersey only once – as an unused substitute in the 1978 European Cup final against Bruges at Wembley.

* Callaghan was elected Footballer of the Year in 1974 by members of the Football Writers' Association, the first Liverpool player to receive the award.

* He was made an MBE in the 1975 New Year Honours List.

Other titles available from Sport Media:

£8.99

'PROOF THAT LIVERPOOL FANS ARE DIFFERENT TO THE REST'
The Liverpool Echo

OH I AM A **LIVERPUDLIAN**
AND I COME FROM THE

SPION KOP

**OH I AM A LIVERPUDLIAN
AND I COME FROM
THE SPION KOP**

Celebrating the history of world
football's most iconic stand

£8.99

"IT'S FRIGHTENINGLY FUNNY"

ALAN
HANSEN'S
STRANGEST
FOOTBALL
INJURIES

**ALAN HANSEN'S STRANGEST
FOOTBALL INJURIES**

Hilarious collection of the most
bizarre football injuries of all time

To buy any of these titles, or for a great range of Shankly and LFC books,
photographs and more, visit www.merseyshop.com or call 0845 143 0001

Sport Media

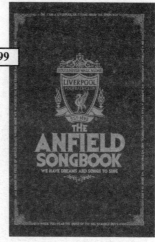